maximus

blueprint
for a dreamer

blueprint for a dream

CLIFF
GRAHAM

emerge
publishing

Blueprint for a Dreamer

Published by:
Emerge Publishing, LLC
9521B Riverside Parkway, Suite 243
Tulsa, Oklahoma 74137
Phone: 888.407.4447
www.EmergePublishing.com

Cover Design: Christian Ophus | Emerge Publishing, LLC
Interior Design: Anita Stumbo

ISBN: 978-0-9907694-5-3 Paperback
ISBN: 978-0-9907694-4-6 Digital E-book

BISAC Category:
REL012120 RELIGION / Christian Life / Spiritual Growth
REL012070 RELIGION / Christian Life / Personal Growth

Printed and published in the United States of America.

contents

ARCHITECT: BRYCE FLETCHER
FINANCIER: TORI GRAHAM
DESIGNER: ALEXIS GRAHAM

acknowledgments

ARCHITECT: BRYCE FLETCHER
FINANCIER: TORI GRAHAM
DESIGNER: ALEXIS GRAHAM

I thank God for this fantastic voyage we call Life in Him.

*My wife Christie, my traveling adventurist,
who has literally followed me around the
world through the thick and the thin.*

*My three full of life daughters:
Victoria, Lauren "Lala" who already
made it home, and Alexis!*

*And our family, friends and faithful partners, with whom we
could not have otherwise embarked together on this journey.*

CHAPTER 1

passion

ARCHITECT BRYCE FLETCHER
FINANCIER TORI GRAHAM
DESIGNER ALEXIS GRAHAM

MOM, I WANT TO GO TO THE MOON!" In the movie *Rocket Man*, Harland Williams played Fred Z. Randall and chased his dream right into the clothes dryer. He had a picture of the moon outside. He climbed in, shut the door, and he called out, "Houston, we have lift off." He started spinning around in the dryer, until his mom opened the door and he fell out. The scene closed with Fred saying, "Mom, I *am* going to go to the moon someday."

WHAT IS PASSION?

Fred Z. Randall had passion. Passion can be defined as "an intense enthusiasm for something, or an acute interest in a particular subject or activity." It can also mean the object of enthusiasm, the subject of somebody's intense interest, or an intense or overpowering emotion such as love, joy, hatred or anger.

Whether it's short-lived or sustained over a long period of time, passion can temporarily self-destruct or even permanently destroy. Whether it is good or bad, misdirected or directed, passion can dominate people's lives. Passion is the vehicle that directs people on their life course.

So you may be thinking you don't have any passion. I say you're wrong. We all have the ability to be passionate, and, if we look at our life, we would realize that we are applying passion towards something. How about when you watch your favorite movie for the twenty-third time in a row even though you already know every single word? *Every* word! Or when you stay up all night long playing a new video game, or learning a new guitar lick, or talking to your special someone, even though your body is screaming for SLEEP!

Back when I was a surfer in Maui (before I became a Christian), my friends and I used to stay up until 1:00am doing the unmentionables. We would sleep for two hours and then at 3:00am, get up and drive from Kihei to Honolua Bay so we could be in the water by 5:00am before anyone else got there. How did we manage to paddle out to six- to eight-foot waves with 12- to 15-foot faces on only two hours of sleep? We were passionate about what we were doing!

No one can say they are passionless because we are all built with passion. It is a motivating force and it's burning on the inside of each one of us!

PASSION EXTREMISTS

The Bible is full of extremely passionate people. Let's look at 1 Kings 19:19. It tells a story about a man named Elijah and his search for a successor. It says, "he departed from there and found Elisha the son of Shaphat who was plowing with 12 yoke of oxen before him, and he was with the twelfth. Then Elijah passed by him, and threw his mantle upon him."

There was Elijah, calling Elisha to follow him, and Elisha was plowing with 12 yoke of oxen! Do you know what 12 yoke of oxen are? One yoke of oxen is two animals hooked together at the neck—two oxen—what most farmers used to plow their fields. Perhaps some used two yoke, which would be four beasts. But Elisha didn't just have three, four, five or six yoke of oxen. He had 24 oxen working! He was a passionate guy! I mean, what do you plow with that many oxen? Do you know how far that many oxen would be stretched out? That's how they pulled wagon trains across the United States! He was a passionate individual, wasn't he?

Here's another story of a passionate individual. I visited my cousin years ago in Oregon and she told me about a girl who chained herself to a tree to try to stop bulldozers from clearing the forest. That girl was definitely passionate, though not necessarily intelligent, in my opinion. Her passion may have stopped a bulldozer from knocking down a tree, but I wonder if she had given any thought to larger environmental concerns. Things like excessive unburned deadfall and overgrowth that occurs without proper forest management. Chaining herself to a tree may have made a statement but what were the ultimate consequences?

A few years later, the result of this young lady's actions and others' became more evident. So many people had fought against harvesting trees that the forests grew unchecked. Due to this unchecked growth, once a fire started, it could not be contained, and millions of acres burned out of control. This girl, and many others, obviously didn't understand what the implications of their actions would be in the years to come.

With all of her passion, what if that same girl had attended law school? Maybe studied forestry and environmental law, the effects of man versus nature and learned how trees could be harvested in a sustainable manner? Wouldn't that have been a smarter, more effective thing for her to do? Instead, it's likely that the same tree she refused to let someone else cut, fell victim to an out-of-control fire. It kind of gives a new meaning to the phrase "adding fuel to the fire ..."

ITS ALL IN THE DIRECTION

You see, passion can either be directed or misdirected. You can determine if your passion has been properly directed or misdirected by looking at what the passion produces. What happens as the end result of passion? Why is it that while one expression of passion may make a powerful statement in the moment, yet another has a more positive, longer-lasting impact?

A great example of both types of passion is found in Daniel 3. It is the story of three Hebrew children and King Nebuchadnezzar. All four of them have passion, but the children have a directed passion while Nebuchadnezzar's is misdirected. The Bible tells us that Nebuchadnezzar built an image of gold 60 cubits high and 60 cubits wide. That's about 90 feet each direction! Building a golden statue 90 feet by 90 feet takes a lot of passion!

Once this gigantic golden statue was built, everyone was told, "As soon as you hear the sound of the horn, flute, zither, lyre, harp, pipes and all kinds of music, you must fall down and worship the image of gold that King Nebuchadnezzar has set up" (Daniel 3:4). Verse 11 states that anyone who wouldn't fall down and worship would be immediately cast into a fiery furnace! Since worshiping a 90-foot-tall golden statue is not based on God's Word, we can use this observation to help create our first passion test: **Is your passion based on the truth of God's word?**

Continuing, in verses 12 and 13: "There are certain Jews whom you set over the affairs of the prophets of Babylon: Shadrach, Meshach, and Abednego; these men, O king, have not paid due regard to you. They do not serve your gods or worship the golden image which you have set up.' Then Nebuchadnezzar, in rage and fury, gave the command to bring Shadrach, Meshach, and Abednego; so they brought these men before the king."

Wait a second. "In rage and fury ..." What is rage and fury? Is it quiet, monotone, gentle communication? Of course not! The King was freaking out! He was screaming! It looked like Nebuchadnezzar was letting loose more misdirected passion. In verses 14 and 15, Nebuchadnezzar spoke to them, saying: "Is it true, Shadrach, Meshach, and Abednego, that you do not serve my gods or worship the golden image that I have set up? Now if you are ready at the time you hear the sound of the horn, flute, harp, lyre, and psaltery, in symphony with all kinds of music, and you fall down and worship the image which I have made, good! But if you do not worship, you shall be cast immediately into the midst of a burning fiery furnace. And who is the god who will deliver you from my hands?"

Before we continue, allow me to introduce the three Hebrew children: Shadrach, Meshach, and Abednego. Their lives are governed by God's truth. They're committed to keeping the first commandment: "You shall have no other gods before Me" (Deuteronomy 5:7). They respond:

> "O Nebuchadnezzar, we have no need to answer
> you in this matter. If that is the case, our God whom
> we serve is able to deliver us from the burning fiery
> furnace, and He will deliver us from your hand, O king.
> But if not, let it be known to you, O king, that we do
> not serve your gods, nor will we worship the gold
> image which you have set up."
> **Daniel 3:16–18**

That brave response took some passionate individuals—individuals with **_directed_** passion. Of course this only fuels more of Nebuchadnezzar's misdirected passion:

> Then Nebuchadnezzar was full of fury and the expres-
> sion on his face changed toward Shadrach, Meshach,
> and Abednego. He spoke and commanded that they
> heat the furnace seven times more than it was usually
> heated.

And he commanded certain mighty men of valor who were in his army to bind Shadrach, Meshach, and Abednego and cast them in the burning fiery furnace … The king's commandment was so urgent and the furnace exceedingly hot, the flame of the fire killed the men who took up Shadrach, Meshach, and Abednego.

Then King Nebuchadnezzar was astonished, and he rose in haste and spoke saying to his counselors, "Did we not cast three men bound in the midst of the fire?"

They answered and said to the king, "True, O king."

"Look," he answered, "I see four men loose, walking in the midst of the fire; and they are not hurt, and the form of the fourth is like the Son of God." Then Nebuchadnezzar went near the mouth of the burning fiery furnace and spoke saying, "Shadrach, Meshach, and Abednego, servants of the Most High God, come out, and come here." Then Shadrach, Meshach, and Abednego came from the midst of the fire and the satraps, administrators, governors, and the king's counselors gathered together, and they saw these men on whose bodies the fire had no power; the hair of their head was not singed nor were their garments affected, and the smell of fire was not on them.

Daniel 3:19–20, 22, 24–27

To heat a furnace seven times greater than normal temperature takes a passionate individual, but would you consider that directed, positive passion? I don't think so.

On the other hand, you have Shadrach, Meshach, and Abednego. These men, only youth really, whom they tried to discredit and kill because they worshiped God in truth, had passion as well. You know what the results were? Everybody in the community were told to worship the God that saved them and a King declared his error. *Now that's the right kind of passion!*

Misdirected passion causes pain, suffering, and bad consequences. Yet the boys' directed passion, in this case, resulted in an introduction to the God of the Universe for all of those people. This brings us to the second test: **Does your passion glorify God and cause others to know Him?**

PICKING UP GOD'S PLANS

We already determined that we can all be passionate, but perhaps you still insist you don't have any passion. I suspect that it is simply because it has been misdirected. So how do we get directed passion?

Let's return to the story of Elisha.

In 2 Kings 2:9, Elisha was following Elijah. As Elijah was getting ready to be taken up into heaven, he asked Elisha, "What may I do for you, before I am taken away from you?" The passionate individual we know Elisha to be then said, "Please let a double portion of your spirit be upon me." The guy who was plowing with 12 yoke of oxen and hanging out washing the hands of the prophet said, "Give me twice of what you've got!" So Elijah responded, "You have asked a hard thing. Nevertheless, if you see me when I am taken from you, it shall be so for you; but if not, it shall not be so" (2 Kings 2:10).

The story continues:

> "Then it happened, as they continued on and talked, that suddenly a chariot of fire appeared with horses of fire, and separated the two of them; and Elijah went up by a whirlwind into heaven. And Elisha saw it, and he cried out, 'My father, my father, the chariot of Israel and its horsemen!' So he saw him no more. And he took hold of his own clothes and tore them into two pieces."
>
> **2 Kings 2:11–12**

The first thing Elisha did was he tore his own clothes into two pieces. To people, young or old, your clothes identify who you are. Hence the saying: "The clothes make the man."

When Elisha ripped off his own clothes, he was ripping off his own ideas and his own ways. He wanted *directed* passion. After Elisha tore his clothes into two pieces, he took up the mantle of Elijah that had fallen from him and went back and stood in the bank of the Jordan. By doing so, he dropped his own ways, picked up the prophet's ways, and immediately endeavored to follow Elijah's footsteps.

Remember, he said, "I want to do twice as much as you did. I want twice as much as you had!" Elisha was willing to do whatever it took, as we can see by what he does next.

"Then he took the mantle of Elijah that had fallen
from him and he struck the water and he said, 'Where
is the Lord God of Elijah?' And when he also struck
the water, it was divided this way and that and Elisha
crossed over."

2 Kings 2:13–14

Elisha was looking for something bigger than himself to direct his passion. God has created you for a specific purpose and plan also. If you want directed passion, you have to throw down your plans and pick up God's plans.

BOATS BELONG IN THE WATER

Years ago, I was in Croatia on the island of Krk getting ready to launch a small campaign event in the town square. I was trying to think of a way to clearly communicate that God has a plan for each one of us. I remembered that as we drove into Krk, I saw two vehicles on the side of the road. One was a car on top of a big shipping crate and the other was a small motorboat across the street sitting on the road. As we went by I thought: *That car doesn't belong up there and that boat doesn't belong over there. A boat belongs in the water and a car belongs on the road.*

Sure, you may have been able to climb on top of that shipping crate and get that car started, make a lot of noise, *vrooooommmm vroom vroom!*, and wave at the people driving down the road—but you wouldn't get very far! You would have likely gotten hurt and totaled the car if you stepped on the gas while perched up on a crate. The same goes for the boat: You may have been able to climb up into that boat, start it up and make a lot of noise; but if there wasn't any water running through that engine it would burn up quickly.

And when you have misdirected passion, that's what you are doing with your *life*! You weren't created to sit on the side of the road, just making a lot of noise. You are supposed to be doing what you were created for. God created us all unique, wonderful and powerful. But without directed passion, you are exactly like the boat on the road or the car on the crate, going nowhere, and not getting anything done!

Misdirected passion is taking your passion and handing it over to the enemy. Trust me, the enemy loves it. The whole time, he's saying, "Come on, baby; come on this way!" He comes to steal, kill, and destroy, according to John 10:10. And he wants to steal, kill and destroy your passion by misdirecting it. But in that same verse, Jesus said, *"I have come that you might have life and have it more abundantly."* There is nothing like His abundant life, and it is in that abundant life that we find our third test:

Does your passion produce abundance or decay?

GETTING ON TRACK

Now that we've looked at three different tests, here comes the fun part. Regardless of what your answers were, you *do* have passion, and it is real. It is yours. You may just need to redirect it.

You see, everything that you're good at, everything you were created for, you get to use for God's glory. Sure you may hit a pothole in life every once in a while, but God still keeps His specific plan for you—His specific *something* for you to do with the passion that's burning on the inside of you. Discovering whether or not your passion is directed correctly is the first step in finding out what that *something* is!

If you have done the wrong thing with your passion or allowed it to be misdirected, *now* is your time to get it back! You can get it back right now! This isn't a waiting game. Seriously. *Now* is the time to get your passion back.

You have an opportunity to live the way you were created to live. Directed passion satisfies like nothing else. You might not know exactly what you were created for, but somewhere along the way, you have probably tasted the joy that comes when passion and purpose intersect. However, if today you find yourself getting burnt out, now is your time to make the decision to get back on track to fulfill God's plan with directed passion. Say this prayer with me:

> *Father, thank you for putting passion on the inside of me;*
> *forgive me for letting my passion get misdirected. I agree*
> *to put down my plans and pick up yours; direct my passion.*
> *I thank you for your promise abundant life. Amen.*

QUESTIONS FOR REVIEW

1. Think of a time in your life when you are sure that your passion was misdirected, and explain what it was that makes that so obvious to you now.

_____

_____

_____

_____

_____

_____

2. When have you experienced a time of peace, enjoyment, and personal satisfaction?
   a. What were you doing?
   b. How did it affect others?
   c. How was God glorified as a result?

_____

_____

_____

_____

_____

_____

BUILDING THE FOUNDATION

Consider making each question a daily meditation, thinking on it throughout a day and asking God to reveal to you something new about yourself as you do so. Review this chapter during the day through the lens of that question, seeing if anything new or different stands out.

1. What are the things you most enjoy doing or have a special skill for?

_____

_____

_____

2. What do others most often compliment you for?

_____

_____

_____

3. How could God possibly use the items on the previous two lists to bring people to know Him?

_____

_____

_____

so you want to be a giant killer?

(OR PREPARATION FOR PROMOTION)

ARCHITECT :BRYCE FLETCHER
FINANCIER :TORI GRAHAM
DESIGNER: ALEXIS GRAHAM

RECEIVING A GOOD RETURN** on a financial investment these days can be pretty unpredictable. But when it comes to the Kingdom of God, no other investment will give you the kind of benefits that the Bible promises. God guarantees us a 30, 60 … up to 100-fold return when we invest on this side of eternity.

Psalm 37:4 reads, *"Delight yourself also in the Lord, and He will give you the desires of your heart."* So, as you delight yourself in Him, He is going to drop into your heart the plan He has for you and where you are to invest your time, your energy and your resources. As you walk with Him, it will become more apparent that you are on the right track.

People frequently ask me, "Why do you just work with youth?"

My wife, Christie, and I don't only work with youth, but to quote the apostle Paul, *"I minister to the Gentiles and Peter ministers to the Jews"* (Galatians 2:7). Every now and then they cross over and we minister to different age groups, but it's primarily with the youth that God has graced us to work. We are passionate about reaching them! They gravitate towards us and we gravitate towards them. I believe God guarantees us a good investment when working with them and here is why:

> "And it shall come to pass afterward, that I will pour out My Spirit on all flesh; your sons and your daughters shall prophesy, your old men shall dream dreams, your young men shall see visions."
>
> **Acts 2:17**

When the scriptures states, "it shall come to pass afterward," what does "afterward" refer to? It refers to the last days. Would you agree that we are in the last days? Jesus said to the Pharisees, *"Look, you know the times and you know when you are supposed to grow, when you are supposed to plant, but you do not know the sign of the time"* (Matthew 16:3 paraphrased). All you have to do is look around the world today to know that Jesus is coming soon.

INVESTING IN YOUTH

And just who are the sons and daughters Joel 2:28 refers to? They are young people! Your old men shall dream dreams and "your *young* men shall see visions." Isn't it interesting to note that three quarters of those mentioned are young people?

Here's a secret investment tip that Wall Street can't match. In Acts 2:17, Peter quotes from the prophet Joel "And it shall come to pass in the last days, that I will pour out my Spirit upon all flesh …" to indicate God beginning to pour out His Spirit at Pentecost. But note that he concluded the verse from Joel and said, "your sons and your daughters shall prophesy and your young men shall see visions, and your old men will dream dreams."

I mentioned this a second time because it is interesting that the second time we see this verse in the Bible, God mentions young men before old men? I believe the Holy Spirit switched that up for a reason. Who are sons and daughters and young men? The youth! I believe God is saying, "Listen, young people are a good investment."

At Rhema Bible Training College, the Bible school I attended, Brother Kenneth E. Hagin, the founder, prophesied that the young people are going to be the foot soldiers in the last days harvest. He also prophesied that the greatest signs and wonders are going to be done through young people ages 14 through 25. In war, who goes to the front lines? Is it the 60 and 70-year-olds? No! They are the ones who strategize and make the plans for the young soldiers to carry out.

I believe that we need captains for our foot soldiers. We need leaders to help direct them in the way they should go. But I'm telling you, the foot soldiers are the 14 through 25-year-olds. It's the youth who the Lord is sending! They're willing to take steps that adults are not willing to take.

QUALITY LEADERS NEEDED

Because we know that youth are willing to take big steps, we also know that they can head off full speed ahead in one direction, hit a bump and turn sideways. Then they may veer off in another direction, only to hit another bump and spin off in the opposite direction. Youth need leaders to help direct them. God's army has to have leaders; all military branches need leaders.

Youth follow whatever example is set before them. Like produces like and the apple doesn't fall far from the tree. Invest your time and finances into hanging out with the youth that are in your life. Read the Bible with them, not necessarily to them, but *with* them. Telling youth what to do when you aren't doing it yourself isn't going to work. They're not just watching what you do or don't do *now*, they're also listening to what you brag about and what you did back in your younger days.

They hear you when you start bragging about what you did five or ten years ago saying, "Oh man, I remember the days when we used to hang out and how we would party!" They see you in your private moments laughing about it when you don't think they are listening. But what they actually hear is "man, that was so much fun."

But life before knowing God wasn't all that fun. When I lived in Maui, I was a surfer and partier, and after a while it wore on me. One day, I sat down on the beach and said, "God, if you're up there, I want to know who you are." And God began to reveal Himself to me.

Sure, sin may have seemed pleasurable for a season and you

may have even fooled yourself about liking a sinful lifestyle, but eventually there were consequences. After a night of partying and your head hurting, you realized it wasn't worth it. So why brag about it now and suggest that it was so exciting? You don't want the kids around you to want to try it because you did, do you?

As I now serve God with my whole heart, soul and body, it doesn't mean that everything is always 100 percent perfect. The road isn't always smooth. I have challenges and struggles too, but I continue to run hard after God and obey His Word. The Bible says, *"His blessings will overtake you."* It doesn't say that you'll have to run after the blessings; it says they will come up behind you and knock you in the backside. Still, you don' t camp out there; you keep running hard after God.

LEADERS GOD CAN TRUST

One of the first times I ministered on leadership was when we were in Alabama helping a church that had encountered some challenges. I began to ask the Lord several questions. "How do you know when you can choose people to work for you? How do you find qualified people to accomplish the task ahead? And how do you know who should be promoted?" He directed me to Revelation 17:14 that says *"... and with him will be his called, chosen and faithful followers."* There it is! We must lay down a track record of faithfulness for others to follow if we wish to qualify for promotion.

I also asked the Lord how He picks quality people. How does He find pastors? Jeremiah 3:15, "And I will give you pastors or shepherds according to mine heart, which will feed you with knowledge and understanding." That goes right along with I Samuel 13:14: "The Lord has sought for Himself a man after His own heart …" God is looking for those that will follow Him wholeheartedly.

He is looking for people to guide His children and young people are the easiest crop to harvest. They are passionate and can focus with **proper direction**. They still need plenty of encouragement and guidance, but their hearts are open to Jesus. They love Him and are willing to be molded into His image and likeness.

QUALIFYING FOR PROMOTION

Let's look at I Samuel 13, where Saul, the first King of Israel, had veritably blown what the Lord had asked of him. The prophet Samuel said to Saul, "You have done foolishly. You have not kept the commandment of the Lord your God, which He commanded you; for now the Lord would have established your kingdom over Israel forever. But now your kingdom will not continue…" (verse 13–14a).

Obedience matters because God has a plan. He's a God of order and design. Many people think, "Oh, God is just looking at the heart." And they stop there. Well, God looked at Saul's heart and saw that Saul was not obedient.

By observing God's ways, I was saved. I was a surfer living in Hawaii, and watched the waves roll in; I knew that I could set my watch and every couple of minutes there would be a new set of waves. Everything works together. The sun rises every morning and we can set our clock to it. The sun sets every evening, there are tides, there are seasons, and the moon orbits the earth. Everything is set to work together.

God is incredible at managing complexity and He knows what He is doing. He is a bigger God than we think or can ever come close to understanding. He can direct and mange every area of our lives!

It's true that God's goodness abounds toward us, but we shouldn't dismiss how He is looking for people that follow Him closely because of it. David learned to accurately hear God's voice and knew it was the only way he could ever rule Israel. In most estimates, David is described as being between 14–17 years old when God called him. He was a youth, but not your average teen. You'll see in the following scriptures that he was a youth with the leadership qualities necessary to qualify for promotion. But whatever your age, whether that be 7 or 97 or somewhere in between, you too can qualify for promotion.

> "One of the servants said to Saul, 'One of Jesse's sons
> from Bethlehem is a talented harp player. Not only
> that-he is a brave warrior, a man of war-and has good
> judgment. He is also a fine-looking young man, and
> the LORD is with him."
>
> **I Samuel 16:18 (NLT)**

CHARACTER TRAITS OF A CHAMPION

Many of us have read the story of David and Goliath and how David used his sling and a stone to take down a giant. I, however, want to look at it again and highlight the specific characteristics that made David great.

> "So David rose up early in the morning, left the sheep with a keeper, and took the things and went as Jesse had commanded him. And he came to the camp as the army was going out to the fight and shouting for battle. For Israel and the Philistines had drawn up in battle array, army against army."
>
> **I Samuel 17:20–21**

In these two verses, the first thing we see is that David *rose early* in the morning. How many kids are sleeping in until after noon in the summer? Not David! He also left the sheep with a keeper, indicating that he *was orderly*. He didn't leave the sheep with just anyone. He didn't find some random guy walking on the road and say, "Hey, can you watch these animals since I've got an errand to do for my dad?" No! David was deliberate about keeping order. *He did as his father commanded him and listened to authority*.

> "And David left his supplies in the hand of the supply keeper, ran to the army, and came and greeted his brothers. Then as he talked with them, there was the champion, the Philistine of Gath, Goliath by name, coming up from the armies of the Philistines; and he spoke according to the same words. So David heard

them. And all the men of Israel, when they saw the
man, fled from him and were dreadfully afraid."

I Samuel 17: 22–24

After reading further in verse 22, we see how David was
responsible, organized and diligent. He was not haphazard, but
careful with the supplies for the men going into the battle. He
then "… ran to the army and came and greeted his brothers." The
KJV says David "saluted his brethren" which means that he was
amiable, a people person. His salute was a gesture of respect and
polite recognition towards them.

And his outstanding character traits don't stop there. "David
heard" which means he listened. *He listened carefully and was prudent.* Young people can listen; in fact, we can all learn to listen
better if we will apply ourselves.

> "So the men of Israel said, 'Have you seen this man
> who has come up? Surely he has come up to defy
> Israel; and it shall be that the man who kills him the
> king will enrich with great riches, will give him his
> daughter, and give his father's house exemption from
> taxes in Israel." Then David spoke to the men who
> stood by him, saying, "What shall be done for the man
> who kills this Philistine and takes away the reproach
> from Israel? For who is this uncircumcised Philistine,
> that he should defy the armies of the living God?" And
> the people answered him in this manner, saying, "So
> shall it be done for the man who kills him."

I Samuel 17:25–27

Let's picture the scene again: a 14–17 year old young man and a huge battle about to take place. Goliath was mocking the entire army of Israel and there was an opposing army on the other side of the hill. How many of you would send your son into something like that? David had something invested in him, didn't he? He was a man after God's own heart. *He asked intelligent questions, double-checked the facts and realized he was taking a great risk.* He also knew that with great risk comes great reward!

> "When Eliab, David's oldest brother, heard him speaking with the men, he burned with anger at him, and asked, 'Why have you come down here? And with whom did you leave those few sheep in the wilderness? I know how conceited you are and how wicked your heart is ("the naughtiness of your heart" (KJV)); you came down only to watch the battle." (NIV) "'Now what have I done?' said David. 'Can't I even speak?'"
> **I Samuel 17:28–29**

But *David wasn't easily angered or provoked.* He didn't get mad despite Eliab insulting him three times in front of a group of people. Eliab told him he was insolent, prideful and naughty and what did David do? *David responded without backing down, yet didn't aggravate the situation.* Every now and then you must stand firm. Don't be argumentative, but be ready to stand your ground!

The first part of I Samuel 17:30 tells us that David turned from Eliab. Do you know how hard that is to do? David ran a long distance to deliver the supplies and then Eliab, his oldest brother, got in his face and said, "What are you doing here? I know you, you naughty, little, prideful thing!" How would you react? The scripture says that David turned from him. If you want to take down a giant, you don't just run out there with a slingshot yelling, "Yeah, God is with me!" Examine David's character closely and you'll see that he was prepared. He began preparing years before when he was taking care of the sheep.

> "He who is slow to anger is better than the mighty;
> and he who rules his spirit than he who takes a city."
> **Proverbs 16:32**

We're talking about preparation for promotion. So, after David turned from Eliab, "he then turned away to someone else and brought up the same matter, and the men answered him as before" (I Samuel 17:30). He was double-checking, reconfirming the facts and considering the reward for the risk. He considered what he would receive for going out before the giant and the kind of reward for the peril.

> "Now, when the words which David spoke were heard,
> they reported them to Saul and he sent for him."
> **I Samuel 17:31**

Wait, let's stop right here: *The words that David spoke were heard.* David was a Jew. He understood that he had a destiny when Samuel lined up all of his brothers, picked him over the others and anointed him with oil. He knew it, *but he waited to be called!* God certainly wants you in your place more than you could ever desire, but he also knows the right time.

I believe that at times we must push our way through, dive in headfirst and give it all we've got. There are also times to wait patiently, relax and continue working with the Lord. Let God call you and He'll reveal what is on the inside of you. He's searching for those that are ready for His assignment!

Take for instance, an athlete in trouble who becomes the topic of interest. You know the one, the athlete who was plucked too early, right out of high school. Maybe he has talent and works really hard, but does he have character? That's the question. A few years later, if his antics are ripping him to pieces and making him a laughingstock, the answer is "No." Wait until God promotes you; until he calls you. He knows what He needs to develop in you first.

> "Then David said to Saul, 'Let no man's heart fail
> because of him; *your servant* will go and fight with this
> Philistine." And Saul said to David, "You are not able to
> go up against this Philistine and fight with him, for you
> are a youth, and he a man of war from his youth."
> **I Samuel 17:32–33**

David honored the leader and humbled himself. He wasn't disrespectful as he proposed his vision. He could have said, "Don't you know who I am? Samuel came and anointed me, just like he anointed you!" But how does he respond instead?

But David said to Saul:

> "*Your servant* used to keep his father's sheep, and
> when a lion or a bear came and took a lamb out of the
> flock, I went out after it and struck it, and delivered the

lamb from it's mouth; and when it arose against me, I caught it by its beard, and struck and killed it. *Your servant* has killed both lion and bear; and this uncircumcised Philistine will be like one of them, seeing he has defied the armies of the living God." Moreover David said, "The Lord, who delivered me from the paw of the lion and from the paw of the bear, He will deliver me from the hand of this Philistine." And Saul said to David, "Go, and the Lord be with you!"

I Samuel 17:34–37

Do you understand what David was doing here? He provided his resume, listed his job qualifications and kept repeating about the paw of the lion and the paw of the bear. *He over communicated.* That's a leadership quality right there. He listed victories and gave proof of why he believed he could be successful.

David *rolled up his sleeves and got his hands dirty,* when he caught the bear by the beard. He jumped right in and got to work on the job in front of him. People may be quick to say, "I want to help you!" until they're asked to clean the toilets. You have to be willing to roll up your sleeves like David and do the dirty work.

In verse 36–37, David *restates his resume* and *lays out his plan.* "I killed the lion and the bear and this Philistine will be like one of them, seeing he has defied the armies of the living God." He reiterated his plan of action and then put his trust in the Lord. "Moreover, David said, 'The Lord who delivered me from the paw of the lion and the bear will deliver me from the Philistine.' And Saul said to David, 'Go, and the Lord be with you!"

> "So Saul clothed David with his armor, and put on
> him a bronze helmet on his head and also clothed
> him with a coat of mail. David fastened his sword
> on his armor and David tried to walk for he had not
> tested them. And David said to Saul, "I cannot walk
> with these, for I have not tested them." So David took
> them off.
>
> **I Samuel 17:38–39**

Picture David as he attempts to put on Saul's armor and then "tried to walk." He didn't run with the armor; he *simply tried it out first*. He let Saul know that he couldn't walk with the armor since he hadn't proved it. He didn't just go ahead and use Saul's battle plan, but was uniquely used by God. So although David *was teachable and willing to "look at" another man's battle plan*, he ended up doing it the way he knew how, the way he had tested and proved to himself. He had a plan that was uniquely his and he knew would succeed.

Many times we can misinterpret the actions of young or seemingly inexperienced people. They often time seem either gung-ho with no plan or unwilling to accommodate outside advice. But don't dismiss them so easily since God created only one of them and only one of you, so individualistic that your fingerprints prove it! Be holy and walk with God, but be yourself. I believe uniqueness is good, but even better when it is done according to the Bible.

God has a specific plan and purpose for your life. The only way to fulfill that plan is by giving your whole heart to Him. He doesn't care where you've been or what your past looks like. He has forgiven you, forgotten what you did and wants you to use your talents to take Him and the Good News into every man's world, wherever that may be. He's done that with me!

When I was living in Hawaii, my friend's brother-in-law owned an ice cream store on Kauai. Before he was saved, the guy used to go through $1,000 a day (many years ago) using drugs. Then he got saved and God dealt with him about blessing the Kingdom of God. But, he started to have this attitude of 'I have become conservative now that I am saved. I must be a good steward of my resources!' Actually, he just became stingy. He used to blow those drugs up his nose with no restraint. Why do you think God reached down and grabbed a guy like that? It was so He could do something unabashedly great for His Kingdom!

One of my instructors at Rhema said, "To the extent that you partied with the devil in the world, you are going to have to go so much further with God for Him to *'be exceedingly, abundantly above all that you could ever ask or hope for'*" (Ephesians 3:20). It seems that God saves these radical people and their reaction is, "Now that God has changed me, I drive the speed limit' (except when people aren't looking!); and instead of pulling out their wallet to be generous and give, they are now extremely conservative. When God saves those of us that were lunatics for the devil before, He's probably thinking, "If I could get them in My Kingdom, think of what they would do and give!" How sad when instead of using it for the Kingdom, they spend it on themselves.

When I came to the Lord, I was a risk taker—and not necessarily a healthy risk taker either. At the age of 17, I packed all of my bags and tried moving to Hawaii on my own. It didn't work out as I had planned, so I called an uncle and he brought me back to the mainland. Then when I was 19, I took my surfboard and a bag of clothes and I moved to Hawaii with no job and no housing. Today I would do the same for God! If He tells me to go over here or there, I'm going to do it. I have done it several times with a full itinerary in a foreign land and some $40 in my pocket. Now we have partners and support, thank God, but sometimes you have to just GO!

I would challenge you to *simply abandon yourself to God's plan* like David did. He took Goliath in the way he knew how, his tested and proven way, but I believe he also took a risk. Taking down the giant was no trivial affair; it was a volatile situation. David was smart and calculated the risk involved. Remember, the king was watching. David had experience; *he had taken down the lion and the bear*. I'm sure his father had taught him a lot and he had, most likely, watched his older brothers victories and defeats.

> "And he took his staff in his had, and chose him five smooth stones out of the brook, and put them in a shepherd's bag which he had, even in a scrip; and his sling was in his hand: and he drew near to the Philistine. And the Philistine came on and drew near unto David; and the man that bare the shield went before him."

> And when the Philistine looked about, and saw David, he disdained him: for he was but a youth, and ruddy, and of a fair countenance. So the Philistine said to David, "Am I a dog, that you come to me with sticks?" And the Philistine cursed David by his gods.

And the Philistine said to David, "Come to me, and I will give your flesh to the birds of the air and the beasts of the field!" Then David said to the Philistine, "You come to me with a sword, with a spear and with a javelin. But I come to you in the name of the Lord of hosts, the God of the armies of Israel, whom you have defied.

This day the Lord will deliver you into my hand, and I will strike you and take your head from you. And this day I will give the carcasses of the camp of the Philistines to the birds of the air and the wild beasts of the earth, that all the earth may know that there is a God in Israel.

Then all this assembly shall know that the Lord does not save with sword and spear; for the battle is the Lord's, and He will give you into our hands." So it was, when the Philistine arose and came and drew near to meet David that David hurried and ran toward the army to meet the Philistine.

I Samuel 17:42–48

Goliath was a really big guy with plenty of threats and an armor bearer carrying a shield in front of him! He told David what he planned to do with him after he killed him. David, however, remained bold, declared his intentions to the giant and ran at him with his mouth open. David went for it!

Sometimes people have their entire plan all set up, but when the time comes to take action, they draw back. Don't hesitate when you've done all your preparation! When you know it's time to go, just jump in! Sure, sometimes fear will grip you, but you have to push past it.

I remember standing on the beach and looking at the waves when I lived on Maui. I knew my board was too short; I knew the waves were too big and my knees were shaking with fear. And I would talk to myself: "Are you going out?" … "Yes, I am going out!" "Are you going out?'" … "Yes, I am going!" And then I would paddle out and jump in. So, when God shows you what to do, and your plan is prepared, go for it!

Have you ever heard such a detailed account of David and Goliath? This is what leadership looks like. And, like David's account, God has a perfect plan for your life if you turn it over to Him.

> "David had that champion soul. He nailed Goliath right in the head, literally. 'It shall bruise thy head, and thou shalt bruise his heel' (Genesis 3:15). That champion-consciousness is in the soul of the Christian. Being born of God, he is champion of the Son of God and a demonstrator of His salvation. He is the champion of God. He cannot be anything else. 'As he is, so are we in this world.'"
>
> **—John G. Lake**
>
> *(John G. Lake: The Complete Collection of His Life Teachings)*

Saul missed out on everything because he didn't obey God. The way to obey God is to respond when Jesus pulls on your heart through the Holy Spirit. When He tugs on your heart, give your all to Him.

If you say to yourself, "I want to make sure I step up to the next level; I want to prepare for promotion; I want to be a giant killer," then incorporate these points into your life and get ready for promotion. You *will* be a giant killer!

KEY POINTS FOR PROMOTION

Let me reiterate the key points in I Samuel 17:20–50:

1. David rose early. He was diligent. (verse 20)

2. David left the sheep with a keeper. He was responsible and orderly. (verse 20)

3. David went as Jesse commanded him. He submitted to authority, understanding there was a chain of command. (verse 20)

4. David left the supplies in the hand of the supply keeper. He responsible. (verse 22)

5. David ran to the army. He was excited! (verse 22)

6. David still saluted and he honored his brothers. He was amiable; he was a people person. (verse 22)

7. David listened carefully. He was prudent and intelligent. (verse 23)

8. David asked what would be done for killing the giant. He realized there was a reward for the risk and calculated it. (verse 26–27)

9. David was not easily angered. Though he was provoked three times, he rebutted accusations with the facts. (verse 28)

10. David rebutted. David responded without backing down, yet didn't aggravate the situation. (verse 29)

11. David turned. He was able to turn away from the accusations. (verse 30)

12. David brought up the same matter. He double-checked the facts. (verse 30)

13. David waited to be called upon. He didn't just forge ahead on his own. (verse 31)

14. David didn't undermine authority. He intended to serve his leader.(verse 32)

15. David was respectful. He wasn't impolite when Saul proposed his vision. (verse 33)

16. David over communicated. He made sure others heard and understood his plan.

17. David listed his job qualifications with his victories. He presented his resume. (verse 34)

18. David rolled up his sleeves and got his hands dirty. He got to work! (verse 35)

19. David reiterated his plan of action. He was organized. (verse 36)

20. David placed his trust in the Lord. He knew he couldn't accomplish it without God. (verse 37)

21. David was teachable. He considered another battle plan. (verse 38–39)

22. David developed his own plan. He arranged everything in order and stuck to it. (verse 40)

23. David wasn't intimidated in the face of the challenge. Though the enemy threatened and hurled insults, he stood strong. (verse 41-44)

24. David followed through. He didn't draw back or run away. (verse 45)

25. David reiterated his battle plan, even speaking to the 'mountain' looming in front of him. (verse 45)

26. David declared himself a winner. He spoke of his plans to defeat Goliath and his victory. (verse 46)

27. David gave the glory to God. He didn't forget that it was the Lord that helped him. (verse 46–47)

28. David took the risk. After he prepared with all his heart, he was all in. (verse 48)

29. David was committed. Once everything was set up he ran quickly toward the battle to fight Goliath. (verse 49)

30. David went for it and finished what he said he would do!

CHAPTER 3

SOME TIME AGO, my wife Christie and I were in Zurich, Switzerland sharing a meal with some friends in a restaurant called *The Crazy Cow*. It was a fun, eclectic place. Chairlifts hung from the ceiling, cartoonish murals depicting some beautiful Swiss mountains filled the entire wall and various unorthodox items adorned the menu. My friend Gary let me know: "I am treating you; get anything you want."

I opened the menu and noticed that they had snowboards listed on there! Naturally, when the waiter came, I said, "I'll have two of these snowboards and a cheeseburger." Immediately, my friend Gary jumped in. "No, no, no! Not a snowboard, not a snowboard!" he joked. (They really did sell snowboards, as well as Swiss Army knives and watches; but I ended up with only the cheeseburger.)

As I mentioned, *The Crazy Cow* had this fantastic mural, and a thought crossed my mind: *The more I give up to God, the more He gives back to me. Just more and more.* To you that may sound random, but I remember thinking that and then said to myself, "You know, Lord I would love to do a mural like this on a wall somewhere." It was a mural of a mountain somewhere in Switzerland. It was hard *not* to be inspired with all the cool stuff on the walls, and since I've designed and developed a number of youth rooms, I tend to observe and assimilate that kind of stuff.

Fast-forward about a week as I drove cross-country with my family from New York to Bremerton, Washington, where we planned to preach at a youth campaign near Seattle. On the way, we stopped in Sun Valley, Idaho, for a three-day break from our long trip. While there, we ate at a restaurant called "Bob Dog's Pizza." The owner had recently moved to a new location. (The owner's name was Cliff, not Bob—kind of funny how that works out!)

As I sat in Bob Dog's eating a piece of pizza, I looked up at the bare walls and had an epiphany: I envisioned the wall with a mural of the local mountain, Bald Mountain, just like the restaurant in Zurich. I told the owner, "You need some ambiance in this place. You need a big mural here, and then a couple of chairlifts hanging from the ceiling. I can see Einstein doing an Indy Grab on a snowboard and a skier right over here!"

The owner looked at me and said, "OK Cliff. You do it!" I told him we would be back in November (it was August) and that I'd love to paint a mural. It was on! You see, I believe God gives us all gifts and talents. It's been said that our gift to Him in return is how we use those talents.

A couple of months later when we returned to Bob Dog's Pizza, I had sketched out the idea for the mural. Cliff, the owner, loved it and I ended up painting the mural! I also preached to a local youth church, to top it off, for the entire month while I worked on the mural. Since the youth church was having some internal problems at the time, they couldn't afford to give me an offering for a month's worth of preaching.

We did as Paul said in 1 Corinthians 9:18, "I make known the gospel of Christ without charge ..." Now, if they had given me an offering, I, of course, wouldn't have turned it down. But I found out long ago that you can give everything to God and the next thing you know, you'll be blessed **because** of God. Each step takes you that much deeper, and God will challenge you to rely on Him more and more as you continue to give.

I was able to paint the mural on my own time and was paid fairly well for my work, so I was able to preach for free! Not only did the owner pay me well, but I also got sponsorships from some local companies that gave us some equipment. It just happened, the owner also had the chair lifts we were brainstorming about and were able to mount them from the ceiling. I also found a kid (a little plastic kid, that is) for sale on the side of the road in L.A. We stuffed him and put some ski clothes on him. By the time we were done, I ended up with ski boots, ski poles, besides other things to complete the project. It was just incredible! I was really blessed!

Near the end of the project, Cliff (the other one) and I were sitting in his office and off on another brainstorming rabbit trail. I suggested, "You know what you should do? You should blow out this back wall, rent the place next door and put another extension in there for the adults. Then you could have video games in here for the kids." You see, back when I envisioned the mural on the wall, I knew that God had given me something *for* Cliff, so I shared it with him. Fortunately Cliff, even with his secular business, well, he got it.

One day shortly thereafter, I finished preaching to the youth and stopped in for a visit. Pizza Cliff pulled me into his office. He had started work on an intimate restaurant that would be named the Blue Room in the new part of the building. He said, "Cliff, I have got to tell you this. When you guys came into my restaurant and you had this idea, you came in with all your energy and something happened. Something got a hold of me!" He called it "energy", but we all know what was really going on! God imparted an idea that carried His blessing with it, and Cliff ran with it.

So he worked day and night on his end, and I worked day and night on mine. Before we began, the pizza place used to leave the money in the register at the end of the day and make their bank deposit the next morning. After Cliff opened the Blue Room, and after it became the number one restaurant in Sun Valley for two or three seasons, he had to move his office to the back and install a safe. He said, "Cliff, I am making more money than I have ever made before!"

Do you know what happened there? This man, who wasn't even a Christian, was given a word of prophecy and ran with it.

I'm sorry to say, when we as Christians get a word of prophecy, you know what we tend to say? "Well God, if it's You, You are going to make it happen …"—then we do *nothing*! We sit there, waiting, with a "Where-are-you-God?" attitude. We basically sit on our hands.

Listen up. If God is going to be generous enough to tell you that He is going to do something through you, He is telling you that He wants you to participate! If He didn't want you involved, if God was just going to do it on His own, why would He inform you? Do you think He will just accomplish everything so that you can sit back and say, "Wow, what was that?"

No, He needs your hands; He needs your feet; He needs your mouth; He needs your eyes; He needs your … pocket book! God doesn't have a checking account at the local Bank & Trust. But do you know what God does have? He has His church. What is He doing with His church? He's doing whatever His church will *allow* him to do!

I said to Pizza Cliff, "Sometimes the church will get a word of prophecy, a divine insight and directive from God, and they will wait and wait and wait until its time has passed—but I saw you get that 'idea' and something happened in your life."

He said, "It feels like since you guys came, **I have jumped in a river**." Is that the truth or what? I mean talk about a perfectly scriptural response! He said, "My whole life has changed! It's been awesome!"

What I'm asking you is this: once God gives you something to do, what are you waiting for? What are you doing with your hands? Put them to work! Just like Pizza Cliff, the Lord wants to prosper you. Figuratively speaking, we should have to move from the cash drawer at the front counter to a safe in the back office! God wants us to distribute that prosperity for His Kingdom, and maybe have a little fun while we are at it!

WHAT GOD DOES NOT WANT

Do you realize that we all have God-given dreams, ideas and plans to accomplish? When God has made it clear to you: "This is what I have called you to do, this is what I would like you to fulfill," then do not hesitate! If God has confirmed something that is already in your heart, jump in!

I remember one of the worst days that I've ever had was when I used to surf big waves in Hawaii. I paddled out into about a 20-foot wave. Do you know what it is like when you paddle out to the edge of a 20-foot wave? You get on the edge of the lip there, and if you hesitate, you are in serious trouble!

I remember paddling to the edge of this one wave when suddenly I changed my mind about riding it. I pulled my board back, but the momentum threw me over the falls, dropping me 20 feet down! And that's not the end of my story. At the bottom, the 4,000 some pounds-per-square-foot wave, came crashing down on me like a veritable washing machine. Whitewash pounded me down, pummeled me and threw me this way and that! I shouldn't have pulled back. I should have committed.

We do this in the Christian world. We walk along, saying "Oh, God show me a plan, show me what to do! Oh Lord (sobbing), I love you, Lord, I will do what you want. Just show me what you want!" Then He shows us and we paddle out on that big wave, pull back, and get slammed! Instead of recognizing that we pulled up on what could have been the ride of our life, we look at the crash and say, "I guess God didn't want me to go out surfing to-day." What He *didn't* want us to do was hesitate. When it is time to go, we need to GO!

Lets just assume that you have been walking with God; you have been hanging out with God. Doesn't the Bible say "… and the sheep follow Him, for they know His voice?" (John 10:4). If you know the voice of the one nudging you out on the edge, take the leap and go for it! He is right there to catch you. Remember Peter, walking on the water? Jesus was right there to pull him up when he started to sink. Some people see that story as an example of failure. I see a guy that walked on water, even if only for a moment, and lived to tell about it! That is extreme!

EXTREME LIVING DEMANDS PREPARATION

The dictionary defines "extreme" as "being of the highest degree of intensity (extreme difficulty); exceeding what is usual or rea-sonable; immoderate (extreme behavior); or very strict, rigid, or drastic (an extreme measure)."

If you are going to do extreme things, first you have to be in shape. The world calls it athletic shape. This is how it's communi-cated in I Corinthians 9:24: "Do you not know that those that run in a race all run, but one receives the prize? Run in such a way that you may obtain it." If you are going for something extreme you have got to have a goal. You have to have a direction. Paul continues:

> "And everyone who competes for the prize is temperate in all things. Now they do it to obtain a perishable crown, but we for an imperishable crown. Therefore I run thus: not with uncertainty."
>
> **I Corinthians 9:25–26**

What does Paul mean by "not with uncertainty"? It means he has a direction. One translation actually says, "I run with purpose in every step!" Paul has a goal. He is not running with uncertainty; he knows exactly where he is going. When you are living extreme, you have to keep your eye on the prize, fixed on the goal. You need to be looking down the road at the finish line, or at least the next mile marker! Paul wraps it up with this:

> "Thus I fight not as one who beats the air, but I discipline my body and bring it into subjection, lest when I have preached to others, I myself will be disqualified."
>
> **I Corinthians 9:27**

To be in shape, we've got to discipline ourselves. And then we've got to practice—A LOT.

I have a friend who rides motorcycles and even has his own 12-acre track in his backyard. He used to ride extreme, the kind of extreme that sets up a dirt ramp and attempts to jump over a house. When I talked with him about riding motorcycles, he said something really interesting. He said that when he practiced a new trick he had to do it 200 times before he had ownership of the move. Two hundred times! **What if we took that same approach to our faith? Instead of just hearing a message or even teaching a message, what if we would practice what we've heard 200 times.**

I've taught windsurfing, skiing, snowboarding, water-skiing, surfing, wake-boarding and bare-footing, and I can tell you from experience that his statement rang so true. Regardless of discipline, you really do have to successfully practice it 200 times before you have ownership of the skill. That doesn't mean you can't do it. It means you have to *keep* doing it, practicing it over and over and over until you have ownership.

Do you know what ownership is? In basketball, it means that you know that you are going to have a certain degree of success every time you shoot a specific shot, even under pressure! So how do you get there? Practice successfully 200 times. Complete the specific shot 200 times.

A lot of young people think the guys who huck themselves off these big mountains or do things like extreme jumping are just daredevils—risk-takers. While for a few that may be the case, the truth, more likely, is that most of them have had years and years of practice and have established ownership before they "Go extreme."

So let's say you've disciplined yourself and are now in good shape; you've practiced your skill to the point of ownership. What's the next piece of the puzzle? You have to be willing to take risks, or at least what the world calls "risk"; we could also call it "courage" or "faith."

And when I say "risk", I'm not just talking any risk. I'm talking about calculated risk, calculated toward your goals. You take a risk and move forward step by step, and then you practice, you practice, you practice. Isaiah 28:13 says: *"He tells us everything over and over—one line at a time, one line at a time, a little here, and a little there!"* (NLT).

TAKING CALCULATED RISKS

When God started talking to me, I found out it wasn't "Cliff, you have just gotten saved, so I want you to put on a huge campaign and preach to the world." Rather, God would say to me, "Hey, go talk to your neighbor."

Statistics say that only 25 percent of the body of Christ has ever led anyone to the Lord! Just one person! Seventy-five percent of the body isn't doing their job! I weigh 200 pounds or so. Imagine this: What if I found a person who weighs about 70 pounds or so, and then I let them carry my 200-plus pound body around all day? "Come on, drag me! Grunt!" That is what it is like to only have 25 percent of the body leading people to the Lord—one part dragging the dead weight of all of the rest! It certainly doesn't seem fair.

You know why it's so few? Because most Christians think, "Oh, it's out of my hands. God will tell me one day, 'I want you to go take South Africa, or the western part of the hemisphere.'" But that is not the way God works. He's going to ask you to take a calculated risk.

He'll say, "Can you talk to your neighbor?" What if you brought cookies over to your neighbor and just sat down with them, and talked about life? We are waiting for something so huge and grandiose, but God teaches precept upon precept, line upon line. He taught and He continues to teach me a lot, so much through the simple day-to-day stuff. **One of the most important lessons is that we could accomplish so much more if we would just take small, calculated risks!**

My wife, Christie, and I flew back from Europe one year and a scheduled event was canceled. It was August and we decided to drive across the country. Now we had an entire month open. Did you hear that? No meetings! A month is one-twelfth of the year and I had nothing booked.

As we drove cross-country, Christie and I prayed in the Spirit, "Oh, Father God, what's next? What is the next thing to do?" All I was thinking about was that I didn't have the option of taking off a whole month.

Then I started talking about all the times the Lord said to go back to Hawaii. I had lived in Hawaii, so for me it was going home. I started testifying to Christie about how time after time God made a way for me to get over to the Islands. The testimony of Jesus Christ is the Spirit of prophecy, and, all of a sudden, I saw something.

I said, "Christie, I am not saying this is God or not. But honey, we have nothing to do and we have just kissed good-bye a month's salary. So I told her that I thought that God wanted us to go to Hawaii. Do you know how much three weeks in Hawaii costs, particularly last minute?!" Christie quickly responded, "Cliff, it doesn't matter, God already told me we are going to Hawaii."

We drove to California and within 24 hours we had the money to go, meetings set up, and we were fully booked to preach in Hawaii. It was a calculated risk! I could have just stuffed the whole Hawaii idea down and said, "Oh well, it is a nice dream." But I came from Hawaii to go to Bible School. I took a calculated risk back then, so I *knew* this route! I just had to take a step in the direction of the risk and paddle into the wave.

The first step I asked, "How are we going to pay for this, Father?" because we had just said good-bye to a whole month's salary. And that is when, out of the blue, God scheduled meetings for us. We even had an opportunity to take breaks in places I hadn't visited in a long time. Why? Is it because I am so wonderful?

No.

God talked to me the same way He talks to you. You need to remember that when God says "Get up, take a step toward it" that He's not going to lead you to do something dumb. He cares more about your life than you do because you are His child! He has calculated your plan so that when He lays it out in front of you, you can say, "I know my Father, and I have learned to walk with Him." When God tells you to step forward, He's not trying to mess you up. He is trying to put you on the path He has laid out!

So when we flew back from Hawaii and were inflight the Lord nudged me about a young man that kept getting up to go to the toilet. I sensed God's leading and responded to the Lord, "Yeah?"

God said, "Go talk to him."

I thought, "What? What do I do on the airplane? How do I just walk up? He is not even sitting next to me!" But you know that nudging? Your heart is beating real fast and is screaming to you, "Say something, say something to him!"

When we got off the plane, we waited for our luggage while the conveyor belt went around and around. It had been a successful trip. It was fun, we did ministry, and we even got some new ministry partners. I thought it was over, but I was wrong, apparently. God led us to Hawaii and then asked me to do something for Him on the return trip.

The belt came around again and there was the young man from the plane. The Lord said, "Talk to him!" But we were in the airport, and he was getting his stuff! I started walking out, but then the nudge stopped! I said, "Uh-oh, I don't like this." I turned back around and it started back up again. Finally I walked up to the guy, only by then his dad was with him, apparently picking him up. I looked at him and said, "Hey, you don't know me but I was on the plane and I kept seeing you go to the restroom." He said, "Yeah. You just came in from Hawaii?"

"Yeah," I said. "Listen, has anybody ever talked to you about Jesus?" I looked him square in the eyes. He responded, "Ah, I don't have time to listen to this." He was a 20 year-old man with his dad standing right beside him. I said it again, "Has anybody ever talked to you about Jesus?" He rolled his eyes back as if to say, 'You are an idiot.'

Hallelujah!

I am an idiot, all right! I am a fool for Christ! But I knew what My Father was saying to me. I got a little bolder and said, "Is somebody in your family born again?" This time, he turns to me and retorts, "I am Jewish."

Then his dad began to look at me in the same way that he had. I said, "Listen, Jesus has a plan for you and has His hand on you! I believe more people are going to come and tell you this …" And then I walked away. Christie said they were shaking their heads like, "You are such a bozo!"

Hallelujah!

I am a bozo (or a fool) for Christ. I am talking about being extreme for God. I wasn't worried about what they were thinking in that moment because my God was right there beside me saying, "Thank you, son. You did what I needed you to do!" I would rather be where my Father is beside me, even while people are thinking: "You are such an idiot" than anywhere else.

Inevitably, after being here on planet Earth a while, someone is going to think you are an idiot. Why not just confirm the fact for them? Then they won't have to wonder! Seriously, just take the risk! Granted, risks aren't always about looking like a bozo, but sometimes it is what the risk requires.

Look, when God talks to you and says, "Can you tell them about me?" Do it! It shouldn't matter that you happen to be in the LAX airport and that it's a Jewish guy who *might* get offended. If our Father tells us that the guy needs to know Jesus, then the guy needs to know! What are we talking about? Call it calculated risk, faith, courage or bravery!. I put them all in the same category.

GENUINE FAITH

In 2 Timothy 1:5 (NKJV) Paul says to Timothy, "When I call to remembrance the genuine faith that is in you, which dwells first in your grandmother Lois, and your mother Eunice, and I am persuaded in you also ..." Do you know how that phrase "genuine faith" is translated in the King James Version? It reads, "the unfeigned faith." Now we don't use that word much today but to "feign" means to put on a show or pretend. It means artificial! If God says that you can have a genuine faith or an unfeigned faith, is it possible that you could also have "un-genuine" faith?

People are looking for genuine faith; they are looking for examples of faith.

Come on! How about if we just live this thing? Since God said in the Bible that I can do this, and since I have learned to follow His Holy Spirit, and if I believe that His Spirit is guiding me now, then I can (and should) do what He says to do!" God doesn't want fake faith!

A lot of us have more faith than we are even willing to give ourselves credit for. We just have to step out. During my time living in Hawaii, I moved to the North Shore of Oahu because I was asked to leave a church. Yep—you read that right. I was asked to leave because of what I was saying to the youth. Do you know what I was telling them? I told them that God could speak to them. (AHHH!) I said that the God of the Universe could speak directly to them, so I was asked to leave.

The pastor pulled me aside and said, "How many times has God spoken to you?" I said, "Well, He spoke to me one time in an audible voice or maybe two times …" He said, "I think if He spoke to you two times, you would know!" I responded, "Well, I don't know. I'm just a baby Christian." He said, "We would like you to leave the church. People think you are wrong and they think you have problems."

Well, okay. Maybe I did have problems, but Hallelujah! Anyway, when the pastor asked me to leave, I moved up to the North Shore where I rented a bed at a youth hostel owned by a guy named Mark Foo. He had this big guy named Richard managing the place, and after a little while, as always happens, my faith started coming out. One day Richard ordered me to "stop talking to people about Jesus!" I replied, "Hey, people are asking me questions. What exactly am I supposed to do? Not answer them?" He exploded, "I am going to kick you out. Stop talking to my people. Stop talking to my workers. Stop talking all about Jesus!"

This was a surfer hostel I was staying in. We paid 10 bucks a day while we surfed all day. I was doing airbrush work on the side to pay my rent. One morning Richard came out and saw me witnessing to a guy, while others at breakfast were asking me questions they had about the Bible. Richard came up and said, "I am *so* sick of you!" Fortunately, I knew he still wanted my 10 bucks a day, so he didn't kick me out. In time, I moved out on my own terms, and eventually headed to the mainland to attend Rhema Bible Training College.

Fast forward two years later. I returned to Hawaii after Rhema and I visited Oahu. I was on a bus to go visit a church that I used to attend and guess who I ran into? Immediately upon seeing me,

Richard exclaimed, "Cliff, I got born again! I got born again! I am going to church now!" He was practically drooling on me in the bus! I sat there thinking to myself, "The bigger they are, the harder they fall ..."

Sometimes the people you are talking to about Jesus respond negatively. It may even seem like you are scaring them or offending them, but it may be because they are close to making a change in their life!

But then there are others; I've talked to and watched a fair share of California druggies in my time come. (I'm sure the drugs matter more in this than the state they are from, but hey, it's my experience.) When you try to talk to them about Jesus, they respond, "Well, that is what's good for you. If it works for you, that is wonderful. Ten years later that same person is singing a different tune, eyes bugging out of their head, saying, "Man, I need some help!" They look at you and wonder, "How come you still look okay?

They have forgotten that you told them about Jesus 10 years ago. They remember what they said didn't work for them, but they aren't willing to admit yet that they need what you have—Jesus. "Well, what works for you is good for you but for me, well ... I'm trying something else now." Listen, we need to keep living with consistency if they are going to see the difference God has made in our lives. It doesn't mean you are never going to hit potholes, but the trend over time needs to be progress and promotion in God, not decay and decline.

People are looking for concrete evidence. In James 2:18 it's written: "Show me your faith without your works and I will show you my faith by my works." When you keep moving forward with the Lord, you are going to produce evidence like a tree produces fruit. You are going to leave fruit behind. You are going to have results and leave a legacy.

Fruit is not about looking back and saying, "I did this" or I did that." We need to keep our eyes looking at what's ahead, at the next goal. We need an attitude of "I am running forward toward that goal!" When you do that, you'll hear people saying, "Wow, did you see what he did?" But you're thinking, "What *I* did? I was just doing what God told me to do." People will see the fruit of your efforts, and God said that people would pick out his true messengers, those who walked in His name, by their fruit (see Matthew 7:15–20).

WE ALL START ON THE "D" TEAM

During one of my last years as a ski instructor in Sun Valley, there was a young man named Garret who was getting ready to try out for the U.S. Freestyle Mogul Team. Mt. Baldy is the main ski mountain and is flat on top. There's a ski patrol shack built into the side of the mountain, making its roof about even with the snow after a good snowdrift builds up. On the front side is a Groomer or "cat track", a flat, snow-covered road about 15 feet wide. The chair lift comes up from the River Run side of the mountain, so as you get off the chair there is the ski patrol shack, the cat track, and then the mountain drops off steeply. Garret had been making practice ski runs toward the ski patrol shack and, on this particular day, he was getting ready to attempt a jump *over* it. I was in my instructor's uniform teaching a guy named Philip.

I said to Philip, "Let's stop and see what Garret is going to do." I knew who Garret was because I had seen him for years at the ski resort. Garret got a running start from near the chair lift—a straight, flat run. There is no pitch or incline. Every ounce of speed that he needed he had to make by skating and pushing, but this guy's quads are as big as your head!

He finally entered a takeoff position, launched off the ski patrol shack, flew down and hit the ground right at the cat track. As he hit the edge of the cat track, one ski flew off. Almost instinctively, Garret landed the jump on one foot and skied down with one ski.

While I sat there amazed, a girl named Holly, who used to be on his ski team, turned to me and said, "Can you believe what Garret does now? When we were all on the D team [development ski team], he was never the crazy one. Everyone would try to show off to everybody and throw themselves off these big jumps, but he would come up and do a little jump and land it. And then he would try the next time and do a slightly bigger jump and land it. And then he would do a bigger jump and land it." Apparently all those little jumps had taught Garret how to do *one* thing really well—land his jump and ski away, even if it meant having to pick up some equipment later!

So take some calculated risks in life! You may attempt to do something and find that you land it. You can say, "Okay Father, I'll try this." I believe that is how God teaches us. "Oh, I did it! Cool!'" Then He says, "Okay, step up one," and you say, "Okay, I did that! What's next?" Then He says, "Here, step up again." And you surprise yourself again.

You continue doing that and soon God brings you up to the top of the mountain, points to the place that everyone else thinks is impossible, and says, "Jump!"

And you do. And you land it.

And everyone is amazed, saying, "How did he do that?"

Those who do the extreme keep attempting to rise to the next level. They keep doing it, and then they get it down to where they are confident doing it, whatever "it" is. They don't just launch off the roof, saying "Yeah! Look at me!" and then smack into the cat track and break their legs! People really do take calculated risks because they are in shape and have the discipline to continually practice. But they add one more thing to the mix; they know how to live beyond themselves.

LIVING BEYOND YOURSELF

What do I mean by "living beyond yourself?" I mean that to be extreme, you have got to be willing to step beyond your own fear. In 2 Timothy 1:7, "God has not given us a spirit of fear, but of power, love and of a sound mind."

Do you know what fear is? Fear is a crippler! There have been plenty of times when God has told me to do something, but my flesh didn't feel like going in that direction. Was it because I was questioning who was speaking to me? No, I knew the voice of God. I simply wasn't willing to act on it because of fear. You, too, know the voice of God. You do.

The question is: when He does speak to you, will you act on it?

When I first moved to Maui, I had a six-foot surfboard. I am about 6'3." My board was really small for me. The shorter the board, the quicker the response but it is less stable, especially in bigger waves. I lived in Kihei, on the southwest side of the island, and I would have to travel about 15 miles to get to Ho'okipa, the north shore, where the big waves were.

I explained in the last chapter how one day I made it there with my short little board in tow. I remember standing at the paddle out spot with my knees shaking. I'm not talking about a figure of speech. I mean, they were literally shaking from fear! I had to talk myself into going in the water.

"Am I going out?

Yes, I am going out!

Am I going out?

Yes, I am going out!

Am I going out?

Yes, I am going out!"

I also talked myself into paddling out because I knew what I was facing was a big deal. I didn't have the right-sized equipment but it wasn't unsafe. I had practiced plenty on smaller waves and knew in my heart that I could do it. I still had to overcome my fear because making my short board work in those waves would take everything working right, and I knew that wasn't necessarily guaranteed!

There were times when I went out and was pounded by the waves, but there were also times when I'd catch that amazing ride. To have a chance at "catching that ride," you have to overcome fear! That is what I meant when I said you have got to live beyond yourself. When you know you have practiced then go ahead and take a step out and go for it!

When you know in your heart what to do, it's time! I am not talking about going out and setting up an evangelistic outreach in the city center, having no permits and getting arrested for disturbing the peace. No, start out by talking to your neighbor. Go talk to your friend that God has been nudging you about for so long. You know the one. The friend you haven't gotten up the nerve to share Jesus with.

"Hey, tell them about Me. Tell them I have a wonderful plan for their life!"

God will reward your risk. Even though I went over the falls, I still turned my board around and went out again, thinking, "I have to do it again!" The reward for trying again and succeeding made the pain of past failures even more worth it! Just as the thrill of catching the wave was a reward for paddling out again, God also rewards those who serve Him.

At times in my life, I've come across as kind of an idiot to others, I'm sure. How, you might ask? Well, I was kind of an extremist before I got saved. When I first moved to Maui, I quit a job just because the swells were up for three weeks. There were 18-foot faces, summer swells and I just couldn't stop surfing. I was a fanatic.

When I got saved, I kept my fanatical attitude. That's how we should be. When God said, "I want you to quit that job because I have somewhere for you to serve," I did it. Since I did it when I was a surfing fanatic, it wasn't that hard to follow God's lead when I became a Jesus fanatic.

Why is it that we can be total idiots for the devil, and then once we get saved, we pull back and get all quiet about God? Remember that guy that was stupid and wasted a $1,000 a day on drugs? He wasn't holding on to his money with an iron fist then.

"Oh, but now that I am a Christian, I am wise with my money." I'm sure you've met *that* guy. What about when the Father nudges *you* as you sit there in church and he says, "Give $1,000 to that project."

The guy that was wild before he got saved now thinks, "No, no, that is not wisdom. I will put in my customary five dollars and then go ahead and buy a new couch for my wife to honor her." Sure, financial wisdom has its place, and I'm not advocating craziness, but let's keep our Heavenly perspective! If you were willing to throw away a grand at a party before you got saved, you should be as excited at the opportunity to invest a grand into something God is doing to reach the lost! Why do you think He gets extreme people saved?

My opinion is that He needs risk-takers for the Kingdom. We have enough quiet folks! He needs some voices willing to cry out in the wilderness, not just to be crazy and loud, but for a purpose! Why haven't we evangelized this planet yet? God doesn't want all the wars, poverty and pain that are going on here. He wants us to come home to Him and walk the streets of gold. He wants us to enjoy all that He's prepared! But before that can happen, we'll need some bold people proclaiming His gospel down here!

When I left Bible school, I had several friends and acquaintances that were prepared for ministry and full of ideas. As they stepped out, however, many of them would say, "Oh, but I had a check in my spirit."

Really, they just got scared. Now, I am not saying that they didn't have a direction change, and I realize that I am not their judge. I can tell you of times when I was in the airport on my way to France and other destinations and reminded God, "Father, I have $300 and no other resources on the horizon." When I moved to Maui the first time, I had $200, a surfboard and a bag of clothes. I wasn't a Christian, so I certainly wasn't walking that one out by faith. I just didn't sweat it.

I believe that to the extent that you lived for the devil on the other side, God is going to issue you a challenge. You have to live beyond yourself for Jesus before He can ever show you that He is, in fact, going to do "exceedingly, abundantly above and beyond whatever you could ask or hope for!" (Ephesians 3:20).

Many say, "Well, that's not for me. I am a moderate Christian now. Those were my crazy days!" Perhaps you've heard this as well, "I worship the Lord in my own private way." Oh, really? The Bible says, "Shout unto the Lord with a voice of triumph" (Psalm 47:1). So, are you shouting in your own personal, quiet way? Hum-hum." Do you think that would have torn down the walls at Jericho?

"Everyone shout unto God!"

"Hum-hum."

"Hey, nothing is happening."

"Wait, I think I saw a little stone fall off ..."

God said "Shout!" You have got to shout sometimes! You have got to live life out there! I am not talking about stupidity. I am talking about reaching out to where God is taking you, regardless of what that might mean for you. This is for *us*. This is about extreme. This is living beyond yourself. This is going for it!

Check out Hebrews 10:35–36: "Therefore, do not cast away your confidence which has great reward. For you have need of endurance, for after you have done the will of God you will receive the promise." Further down the page, verse 38 continues: "Now the just shall live by faith. But if anyone draws back, my soul shall have no pleasure in him."

I like how Paul says, by the Holy Spirit, in verse 39, "We are not of those who draw back to perdition but of those who believe to the saving of the soul." Note that they wrote: "We are not of those who pull back." Once you have the plans, are in athletic shape and have disciplined yourself, once you realize the risk and are willing to take it, you *have* to go for it! You've got it all lined up, you're looking fear straight in the face and you shout, "Hey, He hasn't given me a spirit of fear!" (2 Timothy 1:7).

Emotions make great servants but poor masters. When I was scared of those big waves, it wasn't about a check in my heart. It was about my body being filled with fear. I remember standing there with my knees shaking. And you know what? Sometimes you just have to say, "No way, body, we are going (fill in your blank) today." When you get to that point where you can tell your flesh to be quiet, where you start stepping over that line on purpose, then it will get easier to deal with this thing called "fear."

I read an article about people who surf the place called "Jaws" on the island of Maui. The article addressed the challenges of the waves, and the dangers involved. It talked about fear, and that fear isn't even an accurate enough word. I know one of the guys, Laird Hamilton, as an acquaintance. He lived right around the corner from me. He is in incredible athletic shape, and yet even he said, in regards to Jaws being scarier to surf, "You step over into sheer terror."

Wouldn't it be amazing if Christians would say, "Hallelujah! This week we are going to step over into sheer terror! We are going to witness to everybody in town." Can you see that? What do you think you are here for? God needs people who are willing to look at sheer terror and say, "Come on! Let's do it!" You may be wondering if this is scriptural. That is a reasonable question, so let's see.

We've already gone over the story of how David ran at the giant Goliath. Then there was Paul who went before King Agrippa, Daniel was thrown into the lions' den and Shadrach, Meshach and Abednego were thrown into the fiery furnace. How about when the Israelites crossed the Red Sea, Peter walked on the storm-tossed Tiberian Sea or when Jesus went to the cross for us? Yeah, I believe it IS scriptural!

CHRISTIANITY IS NOT JUST A BUNCH OF NO'S

Those examples are extreme, right? Haven't you ever noticed how the youth around you have high ideals? Shoot-for-the-moon ideas? "Well, I would like to be the world X Games Motocross champion." All the while, you are thinking, "Yeah, right. You barely know how to ride a bicycle."

I believe one of the biggest problems people have with Christianity is that they think it's all about "No, no, no! You can't do this, you can't do that!" People tend to think that when they were in the world, they lived like they had free rein. "Friday night, I can stay out 'til 5am! I can do what I want, whenever I want!" They think to become a Christian means God takes away things. "You can't do this, and you can't do that." Do they feel like their world gets smaller and smaller? As they feel pushed up and crammed into the "no-zone" do they tend to think, "Man, this whole 'living for Jesus' thing is no fun"?

I believe the Lord wants us to see it differently. Let me tell you how He revealed it to me.

Have you heard of the Monaco Grand Prix in Monte Carlo? A close friend gave us an apartment (or flat) several times to check it out. You should see those guys climb into their Ferrari Formula 1 cars. The doors don't open because they are welded shut. Those guys still climb in. It is hot, sticky and uncomfortable in there. After they climb in, they get strapped in super tight with five-or six-point harnesses. The drivers have helmets on and it is already 95 degrees outside. Do you know how hot it must be inside that car? Nearly 120 degrees or thereabouts! Then the drivers take off as fast as the car and their *skill* and *training* can take them!

That's where we miss it. You want to jump in and go full throttle, but it seems as though God is holding you back, restricting how fast you can go. If that is you, it's probably for your own safety. If you get out of control in a Formula 1 racecar, you could hurt yourself, harm others or kill people. You must know how to drive the vehicle first. God is teaching you how to live this life for Him.

First, He is tightening up the safety harness by tweaking your own desires. Your conscience starts to rub you a bit and you feel uncomfortable. That's only the seat belts. They keep you in the vehicle and help you maintain control. Some people act like they are still on a little, dinky tricycle, "doop-dee-do." And listen, if you fall over and go "boom" you are going what, three miles per hour? No major damage.

But if you get in a Ferrari and get going over 230 miles per hour and down shift from third gear to first, or fourth to second, then what happens? Your transmission goes, you spin out of control and you hit a wall and get smashed. God has got to teach you how to shift. You need to learn to follow His intricate shift pattern. It is delicate. You have to alternate pushing and letting up on the clutch, pushing and letting up on the gas, avoid hitting the brake pedal … and do it all smoothly while buckled in so tight you can barely move—that is if you want to competently maneuver the car and find its true potential.

I believe God is trying to integrate a lot of people and protect them until they are strapped in tight and know how to shift and drive. But it still gets difficult, uncomfortable and challenging. So you know what many people do? They chuck it all, saying, "I am sick of this!" Really, that's when life is just starting. He's just getting ready to promote and advance you! The Bible says that when we are saved, the very same power that raised Jesus Christ from the dead is alive in us. That is a ton of power! God is saying, "I've given you all the power you need, and I want to put you on the track. I want to put you in with other drivers, but first you've got to learn how to drive!" As you receive His instruction, allow the belts to be tightened, and become familiar with His power. Suddenly, you **will** realize that it's like driving in traffic at 200 and something miles an hour.

That's what He's trying to do with us, and that is why He gave us a manual! He has given the instruction, the direction, and the discipline, so we really learn how to drive. Hey, if you're happy going "doop-dee-do" on the tricycle and you don't want to change for Him, okay. You can stay on the tricycle. He is not going to stuff you up inside the Formula 1 car because you'll just end up doing harm to yourselves and others.

How about this one? What happens when you go too far, too fast, and it seems that Jesus has made the belts too tight? You say, "I can't take it anymore. I am going to go party my brains out." All of your friends have been seeing you testify for years about how good God is and now they come back saying, "Look what happened to him! He was so in there with God. If he couldn't do it, nobody can do it." You explode and you take out a whole crowd with you. I think He is looking for people who are faithful that He can send on to the next level.

You see, you start out with a broad base before you come to the Lord, but when you give your life to Him, He begins to train you. The training may make life seem like it is becoming more restricted, but really God is just developing you, checking on you to see how you will respond in any given instance. Then, once He knows you are able to respond to a set of circumstances, He can send you out with His agenda. That's when a Christian's life really begins to open up.

DEVELOPING FOR THE EXTREME

God is looking for people to live extreme, but to be one, you have to determine to develop yourself *right where you are*. You have to let Him tighten up your life. Christie and I have endeavored to do that over the years. For example, we've attempted to never be alone in a car with a single person of the opposite sex. You say, "Well, that's a little bit overboard." Yes, but we don't want to give a place for anyone to ever accuse us of something we didn't do. We are never alone with someone else in a hotel room. We've set up these boundaries around our lives and want to be effective for Jesus Christ. This may be a good time to re-evaluate your life and set up some new boundaries as well. The results of this lifestyle enable Him to let us do more and more. Christie and I simply avoid the opportunity for even the appearance of evil.

When you cooperate and adjust your life, you let God increase you more and more. "Here I am. Strap me in real tight, because once I can start driving that Formula 1 car, it is going to be so amazing!" Sure driving that Ferrari and sweating because of the heat may seem uncomfortable and stressful to many. But the drivers say they actually lose all consciousness of the surroundings as they simply focus on the mechanics, go through the shift pattern, focus on the track, and fly across the pavement at excessive extreme

speeds! You can't pick up that kind of speed on a tricycle.

In review, to live extreme, you must first be in shape; know your passion and develop the discipline to practice. Then be willing to take risks, albeit calculated risks requiring courage and faith. In addition, you must live beyond yourself. You've got to learn to face fear—face the unknowns, the losses and even the successes. Who better to face these with than with the God of the universe? And finally, go for it! Just do it! He'll lead you to victory *if* you'll follow Him.

CHAPTER 4

✝

DEFINE [dī'fin] verb {trans.}1. state or describe exactly the nature, scope, or meaning of; 2. mark out the boundary or limits of.

SEED [sēd] noun. 1. A flowering plant's unit of reproduction, capable of developing into another such plant. 2. figurative the cause or latent beginning of a feeling, process or condition.

Jesus told His disciples a parable:

"Listen! Behold, a sower went out to sow. And it happened, as he sowed, *that* some *seed* fell by the wayside; and the birds of the air came and devoured it. Some fell on stony ground, where it did not have much earth; and immediately it sprang up because it had no depth of earth. But when the sun was up it was scorched, and because it had no root it withered away. And some *seed* fell among thorns; and the thorns grew up and choked it, and it yielded no crop. But other *seed* fell on good ground and yielded a crop that sprang up, increased and produced: some thirty-fold, some sixty, and some a hundred."

And He said to them, "He who has ears to hear, let him hear!" But when He was alone, those around Him with the twelve asked Him about the parable. And He said to them, "To you it has been given to know the mystery of the kingdom of God; but to those who are outside, all things come in parables."

Mark 4:3–11

We are going to focus on verse 13. And He said to them, *"Do you not understand this parable? How then will you understand all the parables?"*

Do you think if Jesus said, "How then will you understand all the parables?" that just maybe He was saying, "This is a key to my Kingdom." I submit to you that He is saying there is something involved in this, that if you can understand this parable of the seed and the sower, then you might understand other parables? As I was studying, I kept thinking "keys to the kingdom … keys to the kingdom."

How many of you have heard faith, faith, and more faith? And many times people say, "I am sick of faith, faith, faith!" What's this faith, faith, faith stuff? People talking about faith formulas. Do you know what a formula is? A formula is putting several ingredients together of equal or consistent quantities, mixing them together and shaking them up. Then what comes out? You'll have some type of food, a product, or a desired outcome. If you follow the directions accordingly, it should always be consistent.

Well, I believe Jesus was talking about something different than a formula. Like I said, I was thinking of a key and it hit me. I came to the conclusion that He is not talking about a formula, He is talking about a key—*a key or keys to the kingdom*. What is the difference between a key and a formula?

Many people belabor the point and say, "You are giving me a faith formula." I think sometimes people don't understand that Jesus wasn't teaching us faith formulas. You mix this, this and this and you come up with a certain concoction and then you drink it down and it always does what you need it to do. No, I believe He was talking about keys to the kingdom.

KEYS, NOT FORMULAS

Do you know what a key does? A key opens a door or a portal, so that you may enter into another room or space. And what you do when you enter into that room is really your responsibility. I believe that Jesus has given us many keys, or keys to the kingdom, with faith. And a lot of us are looking for formulas so that we can mix it all up and "guzzle" it down in order to get what *we* want. But I don't believe that is what Jesus was doing. I believe that He was giving us keys so that we could access the things that we need or the places that we need to go *in* the kingdom.

Once we have opened the door and entered in, (and this is where I think some people have missed it) the responsibility lies on us to act appropriately and to be responsible to Him. He has revealed to us the door, allowed us to enter in and given us what we have asked for from Him.

But a lot of people go through this portal, if you will, and then they just kind of go haywire, like "Hey, wow!" And they misuse what God has given them, and only pursue what *they* want.

I believe He is saying, "Listen, I can help you get what you need, the right thoughts, ideas and direction." But then many people, once inside the door, exclaim, "Wow, look at the freedom in here!"

There is a reason why the door was closed and locked up. We have to use what God gave us to get in there, to gain access to His Kingdom. This is about "defining your seed." We read that passage to study the one scripture because I don't want to take things out of context. "Know you not this parable how then will you know all parables?"

Years ago, I attended Rhema Bible Training College in Broken Arrow, Oklahoma, for Bible school. I also attended 'optional' prayer school every afternoon. God put it on my heart to attend just as I would a regular class. I missed only two or three days in the entire two years and the instructor always let me know that I hadn't shown up. When I walked in, the instructor said, "Hey, we missed you yesterday in prayer school."

Her comments were a good confirmation for me because when things were challenging, I would say, "Lord, I need to be working more." And the Lord would respond, "Well if you need to be working more, why you are even going to Bible school?" He was trying to teach me a principle in life, regardless of present circumstances.

At prayer school, I learned another principle that has been repeated by others. In fact, I was listening to a preacher recently while traveling. At some place in the message, the man's wife said he received a word from God saying that, **"Prayer is the currency of the Kingdom."**

It seems to me when you pray or when you *labor in prayer*, it builds up an account for you. When you need to draw on that account, you can. It helps you reach or receive what you need from the Kingdom of God to fulfill the call that He has on your life.

An allegory may paint a clearer picture "When you pray, it's as if you're laying down railroad tracks ahead of you. As you pray and spend time with God, praying mysteries out, praying with your understanding and praying in the Spirit, you are laying a track down in front of you mapping where you need to go. Subsequently, if people don't pray, they get stuck and there's no more track out ahead of them.

I attended prayer school for two years and we prayed about many things. We prayed about the destruction of the Berlin Wall and, a little while later, we saw the Berlin Wall fall. I am sure other people were praying for it, too. We also prayed about the Gulf War and, I believe, during that time of sowing in prayer, as a corporate body, I also prayed out part of my future. After I graduated from Bible School, I went to France for six months.

PRAY OUT YOUR FUTURE

Later on, I returned to the Rhema alumni office, and I talked to one of the directors. I said, "I see myself being a youth itinerant, speaking at campaigns and teaching/speaking in Bible schools." The director sat back on the other side of the desk and said, "There is no such thing as a youth itinerant." He continued, "It sounds like you have prayed out your future but you are going to have to walk some of it out."

I attempted to do the practical thing; I looked through the book of ministerial opportunities available in the alumni office. None of the opportunities seemed to do much for me. A couple of churches kind of jumped out at me, so I took down their names and planned to visit them while I was in the area. One turned out to be an inner city church where I ministered as an itinerant as opposed to becoming their youth pastor, which is what they were looking for.

I began to talk to the Lord, "Okay Lord, I've seen these three things: I have watched my life and have seen that at about every eight years, I reap a harvest. I have either laid something out, or I have walked something out and at about the eight-year mark, I reap a harvest."

And you know what? Eight years later, I was doing youth campaigns, youth itinerating and, from time to time, I was speaking in Bible schools.

DEVELOP, FRUSTRATE OR ELIMINATE

I believe God puts a desire in each of us so we can dream! Unfortunately, as we grow up, some stop dreaming. We see something that isn't genuine and get disheartened. People laugh when we share our dream or make first, second and third attempts at following our dream and fail. But don't stop trying and become convinced of "what is" instead of dreaming about "what could be." Don't become focused on what we see with our natural eyes instead of imagining the impossible with the eyes of our understanding (Ephesians 1:17).

I believe God places a dream inside each of us and we do one of three things; we develop it; we frustrate it; or we eliminate it, outright.

Perhaps this situation is familiar to you. What happens when you just sit on the dream? As you are sitting there, God keeps reminding you of the dream over and over again. Because you aren't acting on God's promptings, the nudges continue to frustrate you until you get mad at your wife, your husband or you yell at the dog! Then what happens? You usually drop the dream. Finally, you succumb to your own self-induced frustration, saying, "Well, I guess God called me to do this other thing for the rest of my life."

No!

Listen, that dream, that passion in your heart, that thing that makes you want to take off running … well, that thing *is* a God thing! If you don't take a step toward your dream—if you don't run at it, it will wane. If you don't embrace it, it is going to frustrate you, gnaw at you and eat at you until you decide to act on it or completely ignore it. Which one are you going to choose? Act on it!

This is **defining your seed.** If you've got a dream or vision from God, how do you get from here to there? What is it that gets you from point A to point Z? Or even D, E, F, G …? What helps you in between those points? I believe Jesus was talking right here about how you reap 30, 60, or 100-fold.

As I said, when I read Mark 4:13, I immediately thought of the keys to the kingdom. I went to my concordance and found that there is only one thing in the Bible that talks about "keys to the kingdom."

> "When Jesus came into the region of Caesarea Philippi, He asked His disciples, saying, 'Who do man say that I, the Son of Man, am?'" So they said, "Some *say* that you are John the Baptist, some Elijah, and others Jeremiah, or one of the prophets." He said to them, "But who do you say that I am?" Simon Peter answered and said, "You are the Christ, the Son of the living God."
>
> **Matthew 16:13–16**

Now watch what Jesus says when he responds:

> "Jesus answered and said to him, 'Blessed are you, Simon Bar-Jonah, for flesh and blood has not revealed *this* to you, but My Father who is in heaven.'"
>
> **Matthew 16:17**

Let me ask you this: If I am hanging around with people (flesh and blood) all of the time, even if they are the smartest, most successful people, then what kind of knowledge am I going to amass? What kind of direction am I going to get for my life? I'd probably get worldly knowledge. We want to be sure to hang out with Jesus to get His knowledge. He gives wisdom liberally to those who ask.

Obviously, Simon Peter spent some time with the Father for the Father to reveal something to him. *We are talking about praying and getting from A to Z!* Let's look at this again. Jesus answered and said to him:

> "Jesus answered and said to him, 'Blessed are you, Simon Bar-Jonah, for flesh and blood has not revealed *this* to you, but My Father who is in heaven.' And I also say to you that you are Peter (which means "rock"), and on this rock I will build My church, and the gates of Hades shall not prevail against it. **And I will give you the keys of the kingdom of heaven**, and whatever you bind on earth will be bound in heaven, and whatever you loose on earth will be loosed in heaven."
>
> **Matthew 16: 17–19**

There are some interesting challenges with this particular scripture which we'll examine. This passage reads, "I will give you the keys to the kingdom of heaven." And He said, "and whatever you bind on earth will be bound in heaven and whatever you loose on earth shall be loosed in heaven." I looked up those words and said to myself, "How is this a key?"

When you bind things on earth they will be bound in heaven, when you loose things on earth they will be loosed in heaven.

I looked it up and we sometimes twist it the wrong way. When you are talking about **binding** on earth, the word means "to tie, to knit, to wind, to form, to make request," and then it is added to the word, "necessary." So it actually means "to affix something" and I interpreted it this way, "affix it to the earth."

Whatever you bind on earth, will be bound in heaven, whatever you loose on earth will be loosed in heaven. When you look up the word "**loose**" it means, "break off, destroy, and dissolve." It comes from a root word that means "melt, put off" and it is compared to another word that says, "a shattering to minute particles."

Many times we pray those prayers, without understanding. (I'm not trying to get into deep doctrine here; I just want to make a comparison.) When searched out, it seemed like binding something attaches it to the earth and it is released from heaven. And when you loose things, it's shattered into a million pieces and disappears. And so I said to myself, "What is this? Keys, what are keys? I want to get to this point!"

Eight years later, I saw what happened and thought, "What did I do? What did I do all that time in between when people would say to me, 'Listen, we see you being a fantastic youth minister in our church! We will offer you a salary, we will do this and that ...'" Well, I would go **pray** about it, and would get from the Lord, "No, that is not what I told you, you know what I told you to do."

Then I began to realize as I looked at my life, that our words have power. Isn't it amazing that Jesus didn't say the "letter of God"? Now I know that we say we are "living epistles" but Jesus called it the "Word of God."

What do you do with words? You speak them. What do you do with letters? You read them. Why does He talk so much about the fact that man should not live by bread alone but by every *word*. Why didn't He say every letter of God? Jesus said, "By every **word** that proceeds out of the mouth of God."

Where does it come from? It doesn't come from the thoughts of God; it comes from the mouth of God. So what are we supposed to do with our words? Think about it! We are supposed to *speak* them! There is something about speaking words, there is something about saying words, there is something about constantly communicating that creates a direct connection with the Kingdom of Heaven. Every word that proceeds out of the mouth of God. And what did He say in the parable of the sower? The sower sows the **word**.

Jesus said, "Simon Bar-Jonah, flesh and blood has not revealed this to you."

WHAT DID HE SHOW YOU?

Awhile ago, I was with a youth minister who was designing a youth café and media center. We were talking during a break of some meetings we were attending and he said, "Cliff, I have this idea."

While he was talking to me, *I saw this picture in front of me.* He continued, "We want to reach the youth in our area and have come up with this unique, kind of café-media place. We want to get computers, do video and we want it to have an artistic flair. *As he was talking, I saw this seed, a big seed. He and his close*

partners were planting it in the ground.

"We began our project," he said. "And all of a sudden, we started to have problems with finances so we recruited a fundraiser to come in and help us. The fundraiser told us that we need to get the community to rally around us since we were trying to reach the youth."

He was able to get the mayor and different key people involved. They came, looked at his seed and examined it. They said, "One of the problems you are having with your seed and the reason you can't get funding is because it is not exactly what *we* like. It has a little too much religiosity. Do you understand what we are talking about?"

I watched the picture change, as I talked with my youth minister friend. Sometimes people think I am kind of funny—like when I am talking to them and even my wife says that I kind of gaze off a lot. But you would be amazed at how many times the Lord has told me little things during those times.

I saw the community gather around him and dig up the seed; they pulled the seed out and they started redefining it.

My friend continued talking, "We have raised the finances from the city, and they are helping us." And then I saw this seed being planted that had very little to do with what they had originally planned. He said their plan was to reach youth for Christ with an artistic flair. But I watched the community come around him, and then they hit a point when they didn't know where to go next.

I saw the community pull the seed out and tone it down to their version of Christianity. The end result was a cool artistic

***place that helped a couple of young people to be Christians.
And then I saw them planting it back into the ground together.***

My friend said, "What do you think?" I replied, "This is what I saw while you were talking … eight years from now, where you originally expected this to develop and have Christians with a little bit of artistic flair, you'll have a bunch of artists with one or two Christians."

He didn't listen to me, but who am I?

I will never forget what happened after he described that in front of me. All of a sudden, it went click. I had already hit my last eight-year cycle mark! And I said to the Lord, "That is why you have had me engage with your plan for me. That is why you, Lord, have me *continually saying*, "I see myself as a youth itinerant. I see myself doing campaigns. I see myself speaking in Bible Schools."

I realized that hanging out with flesh and blood had not revealed this to me but hanging out with the Lord had. He had laid down a clear railroad track in front of me. It was such a stark projected vision that I could see it defined as compared to what the natural circumstances were around me.

STICK TO THE PLAN

This made it very easy to walk right in the center of what He said to do, even though hardships came, finances were low, and even though people said, "What you are doing doesn't make sense to us." But then, all of the sudden, I started seeing it!

I remember people saying, "You know that you could speak to adults and you could probably do a lot better financially." I said, "You know what? I have watched my Father year after year and have found that where the Father guides, He also provides. Breaking new ground may look rocky and it won't always be easy to plant but if you keep on plowing, and you keep on sowing, you will reap a harvest."

Have you noticed that this generation is making way more money than their parents ever thought they could make right out of school? They have more liquid resources available to them, too. Well, what does that mean? It means that the television, music and technology industries target them because they know this generation will spend the money. This is a generation that God can provide resources to reach.

So when He tells you something, stick to your plan, regardless of circumstances. You need to stay focused. The only place He is going to reveal it to you is in those quiet places, where you are consistently praying, consistently hanging out with Him and developing intimacy during that time.

God has given you ideas, thoughts and plans. Put the seeds in the ground and then water them. But you say, "I don't have any money to fertilize it. How do I get from here to there?"

The Word, by speaking the Word! Speak to your seed, define your seed, locate your seed. Whatever you bind on earth shall be bound in heaven, whatever you loose on earth shall be loosed in heaven.

I spoke to *my* "seed" (idea, thought and plan) and said, "I thank you Lord, that you have prepared me for the things that you have given me in my heart. I see myself being a youth itinerant." You know what? Ten years after graduating Bible school, I was one of the three licensed youth itinerant ministers with Rhema. That was about 0.1%! That big seed that I saw in my mind's eye for years, finally had a little shoot spring forth and then there was a plant!

People said there wasn't even a chance, but when you see the shoot then you know there is some thirty, some sixty, and some one hundred-fold available.

I really believe God is looking for people to do some unusual things. Youth itinerating seemed unusual to many people years ago, but it also seemed that the young people were the most overlooked people group in the church. There has been a major focus on the children and, of course, a major focus on the adults, but that transitional age is the hardest age to consistently reach. Most statistics agree that 85% of people come to Jesus before 21 years of age. No stockbroker would ever overlook the 85th percentile as an investment!

I imagine a stockbroker musing, "Let's see, I've got a fund over here that yields 85% and then I've got a fund over here that yields 15%. Let's invest all of our money over here at the 15%." No! They would look at it and say, "Which fund will yield a greater return for my investment?"

The stockbrokers that reveal the long-term investments are those that make the most money. I'm not talking about the speculators, the ones that come in and make their quick buck. The long-term ones will tell you to always invest for the long term even though the returns aren't immediate.

That sounds like youth to me! It may not seem like I'm getting the quick returns like those guys investing in the short-term runs, but if you sat on your Coca-Cola or Apple stock for years, what do you produce? One hundred times return on your money! These people, the ones who invested for the long-term, they have *really* received a return on their investment.

GOD, IS THAT YOU?

Let's address how we know that these are ideas God has given to us. You may have an idea that seems different, but there is nothing wrong with being different. I believe God gives us unique ideas. If we were all the same, we would all be trudging along in the same direction. When I speak of individual differences, I am not talking about rebellion.

So how do we know that what is in our heart is in line with God? What is the first way that God speaks to us? First, His *Word*.

Let's look in Judges 14:1: "Now Samson went down to Timnah and saw a woman in Timnah of the daughters of the Philistines. So he went up and told his father and his mother, saying, 'I have seen a woman in Timnah of the Philistines: now therefore, get her for me as a wife.'"

And verse 3: "Then his father and his mother said to him, 'Is there no woman among the daughters of your brethren, or among all my people, that you must go and get a wife from the uncircumcised Philistines?' And Samson said to his father, 'Get her for me, for she pleases me well.'" Another translation reads: "She is right in mine eyes."

I communicate that often for this purpose: **If God has got**

something unusual for us to do then it's got to line up with His Word. "It is right in mine eyes." Samson said, "It pleases me well." But how do you know that it lines up with the word of God? Well, **first** he said, "Get her for me as **a wife**" (Judges 16:1). But when you look down the road, he lost this lady from his life. Here is the litmus test! If it lines up with the word of God than most likely, it is right.

You'll have to spend quality time with God to find out for sure how to define *your* seed. Most of us are not just going to be able to say, "This youth speaker shared tonight, I was moved and so now I know I am called to be a youth minister also." Well, maybe you are and maybe you're not, maybe you are called to be a children's minister or maybe you are called to help finance the gospel. Maybe God is going to give you a fantastic idea to develop some little thing that you could make millions of dollars. How do you know? If it lines up with His Word, it has integrity.

Look what the Word says in Judges 16:1: "Now Samson went to Gaza and saw a harlot there, and went in to her." Hmm, that seems a lot different than where he said, "I have seen a woman in Timnah of the daughters of the Philistines; now, therefore get her for me as a wife." Let's not get into technicalities here, but we know if it lines up with the Word, that's the litmus test. I am not talking about rebellion, I am talking about unusual things for God. Defining your seed *God's* way.

Look at Isaiah 1:19 and 20: "If you will be willing and obedient you will eat the good of the land." All those years, people were trying to corner me by saying, "We see the potential in you to be a youth pastor since you know how to handle youth ..."

You know why? **"But we have this treasure in earthen vessels, that the excellence of the power may be of God and not of us"(2 Corinthians 4:7).**

I had written out God's plan for my life on paper and had invested time in prayer , year after year. I began to speak about this thing. I worked six months a year at a ski resort and then the other six months I knocked on doors for youth ministry opportunities. I traveled all over the world, beginning with the United States and Europe. Some pastors would say, "What are you doing? You need to sit somewhere and get your head screwed on straight." I didn't get angry with them. I just said, "Father, I see right here it says, 'I will be a preacher unto babes'" (1 Peter 2:2, 1 Corithians 3:1–2).

I continued to find scriptures that defined what I was doing and delved into studying them (see Joel 2:28, Acts 2:17). I prayed even when people rebuked me upside, downside, rightside, left-side and wrong side. I would said, "OK, God, this is what they are suggesting I do. But, for some reason, the more I pray, the more my burden leans toward this direction."

I attended services and watched the power of God touch adults. I stood there and said, "Awesome, have Your way, Lord." I thought, "Wow, isn't that nice that adults are getting blessed."

But then the minister would call the young people up and the power of God would fall on them, and I would start bawling like a little baby. I cried out, "Oh God, pour your Spirit out on these young people, knock their socks off!"

My heart went out to them and it seemed right in my eyes, it pleased me to see young people blessed. I went out on the streets and saw the adults wandering off to work and thought, "Take care of them, Lord, bless them!" But when I saw the youth, my heart really went out to them. *"It seemed right in my eyes."*

SPEAK TO YOUR SEED AND HELP OTHERS

What are you going to do with your dream? How are you going to define it? Let's use the business world as an example. It says in Proverbs 8:12: "I wisdom dwell with prudence and I find out knowledge of all witty inventions." I *find* out knowledge of witty inventions!

So, you know what I began to do? The same thing business-men do when they have an idea to build a huge skyscraper. They plan or draw a model and they sit around and say, "I have a dream!" They build it to scale so they can begin to envision it, to see it. They create a visual focus for their dream, "I see a huge skyscraper right *there* and I am going to have a park right *there*!" They put the model in their office where they can look at it every day and they show it to other people and tell them of *their* idea.

Do you know that other people have used visual models for evil? They found a globe of the world that Hitler had in his bunker in Berlin. It was emblazoned with a huge swastika. Over Russia the chilling words were inscribed in German: I AM COMING. Written over North America were the words: I WILL BE THERE SOON."

Now we know what was happening. Hitler was in North Afri-ca, all over Europe and then he started to work his way into Russia. But he was already looking ahead and envisioned taking over North America. "I WILL BE THERE SOON."

Hitler sat there in his bunker and he did what businessmen do. He had that globe in front of him that he placed a big, red swastika on and said, "I am coming to get you!" I can imagine him speaking to his seed, all for evil, saying "I am coming there soon, I am going to take you and then we are going to move into here."

What do commanders do? What do generals do? They have a well-thought-out plan. **But *we* have access to God and to His plans**! How much greater is our ability to reach our God-given dreams? And we know that Hitler was defeated, in part, because when his leaders brought him bad news, he said, "Ah, I discount that! I will have you shot if you bring me bad news." He wouldn't listen to news if it didn't fit his vision.

But how much more should we take the Word of God along with the dreams, visions and ideas that God has given us *with the motive to help people and bring Jesus to the world,* not simply take over the world.

Years ago, my wife, Christie, made me a little globe keychain. When I was on the road driving, I would pick it up and swing it on my finger and quote Psalms 2:8: "Ask of Me, and I will give you the nations for your inheritance, and the ends of the earth for your possession."

So there I was on the road speaking to my seed, "Father, I want to see the youth of Europe and beyond saved. I also have a little notebook that I bought in Ukraine that has a little map of the world on it. I wrote over Europe: "Souls saved in Jesus name" and put Acts 10:38 on it, "how God anointed Jesus of Nazareth with the Holy Spirit and with power, who went about doing good and healing all who were oppressed by the devil, for God was with Him." Then I wrote "We are coming soon with the Holy Ghost and power" over Mongolia, China and Tibet. This is defining your seed.

You know what little children do? Jesus said, "Unless you become like a little child you cannot enter into the Kingdom of Heaven" (Matthew 18:3). How many little children dream? "I am going to be a fireman! Daddy, get me a fireman suit." They run around putting out fires and announce, "I am a fireman." Or "I want to be a policeman." And they walk around in their little policeman uniform and they say authoritatively, "Mother, I am giving you a ticket for the trash."

But then we become adults and we become so stuffy and we think, "Well, I can't goof around like that." It's OK to have some fun! Let's be child like with our faith and come up with creative ways to define our seed! If the devil used this ideology for his power, and we have the Word of Life, how much more can we do with this key? Jesus said, "Man shall not live by bread alone but by every word that proceeds from the mouth of God"(Matthew 4:4).

Define your seed by posting a picture, building a project or creating a model. Talk to Him, the only way you are going to find it out is to invest some quiet time with Him, "Lord, I can see part of the vision but I need more rail road tracks laid out ahead of me for this to make sense." Just spend some time praying over it.

Let's sum this up: The first thing is define your seed. Find it through prayer. The second thing is do not let people redefine it. Redefining it is like drinking diluted Coca-Cola. It lacks the strength you expect.

God is looking for people who are so focused on what He has for them that nothing will take them off their course. The enemy knows if you don't give up, you will **have *everything you say***. Jesus said it in Mark 11:23 and 24: "…You shall have what you say." He knows that if he can get us misdirected or off of our course, he can win. But we've *already* won!

Winston Churchill was invited once to speak at the primary school he had attended. Part of his speech included: "Never give in. Never give in. Never, never, never, never—in nothing, great or small, large or petty—never give in, except to convictions of honor and good sense. Never yield to force. Never yield to the apparently overwhelming might of the enemy." I, too, have begun to realize that this is one of the biggest keys to winning.

It is persistence, keeping your eye on the goal, speaking to that seed and being a bulldog in life. Grab a hold of that dream, water it with the Word of God, speak to it with the Word of God and fertilize it with the Word of God! **You have to have what God has for you.** *"With God all things are possible, with God I can do it!"* (Matthew 19:26).

Christie and I have dreams of holding campaigns to reach youth. I know it is going to come to pass; we are going to reach young people for Jesus *en masse*. How am I going to get from here to there? By keeping on it in my prayers and not allowing anyone to redefine it. Don't let anybody advise you against God's dream.

I am going to keep speaking to my seed on a regular basis. He dropped in my heart when I went to Bible School to reach a certain number of souls for my life's work. One man challenged me from the pulpit, not even knowing me, to go much higher. I will tell you a week doesn't go by where I don't thank God for those souls. If I told you the number you would laugh in my face! And I will laugh right back *with you* because I believe that God said that is *my* number.

As Bro. Kenneth Hagin said, **"It is better to shoot for a hundred percent and get half way there than to shoot for zero percent and get all the way there."**

CHAPTER 5

what's all this about storms?

IT WAS A 20-FOOT FACE DAY at Ho'okipa, and I'd never ridden that big of waves. I'd dreamed about surfing those big waves and even bigger and that was my first opportunity: board, powerful waves and seemingly the right time.

However, I was under gunned, meaning I didn't have the right equipment for the waves as I went out. I had borrowed my board from Johnny and then while out in the surf he asked me to trade the board with a friend so he could try it. Now I was on an unfamiliar board in the biggest waves I'd ever attempted to ride.

I clearly remember the wave as I paddled into it. This wasn't just a crest forming into a giant wall 20-feet tall. It was like being on the outside of a building and getting ready to ride it. I pulled back the board expecting to just get out, but the momentum of this 20-foot "building" didn't stop and I was catapulted like a kid's toy in the washing machine, on *extra wash cycle*!

I didn't have the experience, know how or equipment for those sized waves but that didn't mean I was done surfing. I would live to charge the waves another day.

The Bible in the Gospel of Matthew gives an amazing account of Jesus overcoming natural laws during a raging storm on the Tiberias Sea. It could have been a disastrous night, but a rather emboldened Peter stepped out of the boat and followed Jesus. The recount of it is as follows:

> "But the boat was now in the middle of the sea, tossed by the waves, for the wind was contrary. Now in the fourth watch of the night Jesus went to them, walking on the sea. And when the disciples saw Him walking on the sea, they were troubled, saying, "It is a ghost!" And they cried out for fear. But immediately Jesus spoke to them, saying, "Be of good cheer! It is I; do not be afraid." And Peter answered Him and said, "Lord, if it is You, command me to come to You on the water." So He said, "Come." And when Peter had come down out of the boat, he walked on the water to go to Jesus."
>
> **Matthew 14:24–29**

Storm: *noun.* A violent disturbance of the atmosphere with strong winds and usually rain, thunder, lightning, or snow.

"These things I have spoken to you, that in Me you may have

peace. In the world you will have tribulation; but be of good cheer, I have overcome the world" (NKJV John 16:33).

The word tribulation, also translated "trouble" is defined as follows: **1.** a pressing, pressing together, pressure; **2.** metaph. oppression, affliction, tribulation, distress, straits.

Unfortunately, storms, tribulations and troubles in life are going to come. Jesus told us they *would* come. He also said, "Be of good cheer, I have overcome the world." Be happy, I have won! Professional fishermen realize that there are storm cycles. Some seasons are normal or average and other seasons are below or above average. That doesn't mean that the fisherman stops fishing. Instead, he learns to anticipate and prepare for certain storms or cycles. He learns how to live in victory in the midst of the storms.

Since storms are coming, what can you do about them so they don't derail your dream? Sometimes, as Christians, we become too focused on the origin of the storm (or trouble) in our lives. God sent down His Son from Heaven to die for us so we could have a personal connection with Him. When the storms of life come, stay connected to Him. He cares about us. 2 Peter 1:3 states it clearly: "He cares about all things that pertain unto life and godliness."

Did you notice that it says *life* first? God understands that there are issues down here. *He* put us down here in this earth-suit. God knows better than you do that this earth suit needs to be maintained. And because He knows, He put it right there in scripture: "… all things that pertain to life and godliness."

He knows you have needs to live here and He cares about you! He cares that you are in connection with Him and communicating on a regular basis. He wants to help you and guide you through the storms.

> "However, when He, the Spirit of truth, has come,
> He will guide you into all truth; for He will not speak
> on His own authority, but whatever He hears He will
> speak; and He will tell you things to come."
>
> **John 16:13**

When storms are on their way, He can warn you, tell you what to do, where to go and how you can be safe. But that information isn't just for you. He guides you so that you can help others. And sometimes we do that right through the storms of life. As you publicly testify that the Lord will take care of you, whether small or large, people watch and see your confidence in Him! They may think you're crazy until your connection with Him provides help for them also. It doesn't matter if they think you are crazy. Truthfully, what matters is who we are on the inside.

He can give you victory in the midst of the storms. For instance, immediately after a close family member passed, I had to return to Hawaii. This happened to be during Christmas break and the airlines said that all flights that I could afford were full. It looked like it was impossible to return for a reasonable amount of money. However, in my quiet time the Lord led me on how to get back to Hawaii. I called back and there just happened to be an opening on a blackout date, something the agent said was never done. I was able to purchase the ticket for a reasonable amount of money.

The way He informed me of that is no different than Him

helping you in your situation. When people see you go through storms victoriously, they'll ask how you accomplished it. You can tell them that it wasn't you. You were cooperating with God and He showed you what to do. Don't take the credit. They need to know that He can do the same for them.

That is what one missionary did. He had a dream to take the Gospel to unreached people groups. He not only prepared for a storm, but God guided him right through one. The book entitled, *Peace Child: An Unforgettable Story of Primitive Jungle Treachery in the 20th Century (latest listing 2005 Amazon)* by Don Richardson is an account of a missionary called to an island people group called Sawi in New Guinea. This missionary went to try to find the key to help a cannibalistic tribe and teach them about Jesus Christ. The tribe was incredibly treacherous, to the point that they actually **loved** treachery. They believed that the best thing that could happen was for somebody to brag about how treacherous they had been.

They would fatten up their 'guests' by frequently and methodically inviting them to dinners and other feasts. Their method was to befriend someone, fatten them up and just when the guest thought they were good friends, they would kill them to see the look on their face as they were being betrayed.

Now think about it, this is the vileness of humanity. They described the victims shock and suffering with such relish. When the missionary told the tribe about Jesus, do you know whom they identified with? They liked Judas best and said, "He is a man like us! He sold out his best friend." This is the actual account recorded in the book. So, the missionary sought the Lord about how to best explain the gospel, the Good News, particularly since they only loved and sought after treachery.

Upon further exploration, this missionary discovered that when a Sawi did something treacherous to someone, then a member of his family was obligated to exact revenge. Honor bound, if you want to call it that. That is oxymoronic! So, somebody in the other family would befriend a person, fatten them up and kill them. Then they sat around the fire and relayed about how treacherous they had been. And then someone in the first family was 'honor bound' to continue the vicious cycle.

In order to stop this process, they had to take a baby child, a young child, and give it to the other tribe. They called that baby a "peace child." They took the peace child from one tribe to the other and then the person became family. Someone in the family would actually have to give up their baby and say, "Here, take our child, he will be the peace child." But ultimately, they killed the "peace child" for the price of what had happened to them.

With this, the missionary had finally found the key interwoven in their vile process of life. He said to them, "Jesus is the ultimate Peace Child! Once you accept Jesus, He has already been killed, He has already been crucified and He has already finalized the payment. Once you accept Him, we are all brothers and sisters!" God built into the fabric of their culture, the eternal answer to their cycle of storms. It was Jesus! He was the key that broke that cycle!

Why did I relate that story to you? Because when storms come, people need help. They really need help! The storm may have passed **you** by, but there are others that are still hurting. They are thinking, "When is the next storm going to come? What is going to go wrong next? What trouble may happen to us?" Christie and I have been through many storms over the years and we know that there is hope in the midst of them! God may not have been the author of those storms, but He can use them. We have learned how to live in victory in the midst of the storms. We have the victory through the Peace Child, Jesus!

> "But thanks be to God, who gives us the victory
> through our Lord Jesus Christ."
>
> **I Corinthians 15:57**

That scripture says He *gives* us the victory! If we don't have it, is it possible that we aren't taking it? We have to accept something that has been given, reach out and take it. He told us how to receive it in His will, the Bible … His last will and testament. Sometimes we have to charge the storm. Let's say we have a challenge, a storm or a tribulation. We have to search His will and find out what is available to us.

We shouldn't give more validity to a man's trust and will than we give to His will. After I graduated Bible school, I volunteered at a church in the south of France and a friend helped me get a temporary job in a trust office in Monte Carlo, Monaco. They needed someone to file papers for a couple of weeks and since I was preparing to return to the USA shortly, it was perfect. One day I let Linnane, my friend that got me the job, know that I didn't quite understand trusts. I understood what a will was, but I wanted a deeper understanding. She suggested I stay for an extra hour and read over a particular trust. The lady in charge of me, Anne, was certain that I wouldn't find it interesting. She said, "You aren't going to like that because it is boring, totally boring." I said, "I'd like to know what I am involved with here." Now remember, I'm correlating this with how to search out His will in the midst of a storm.

So I sat down and started reading the trust. In a nutshell, here is what I gleaned in that hour. Say Mr. John Peterson left to his inheritors, Jean, Judy and Joseph, their entitled money every year that the trust company allots, a set number every year. It stated that the monies would be automatically distributed to them as deemed fit. I suppose by the father, the trust officers and according to the current standard of living that they are accustomed to, I'm guessing.

I was really interested at this point in studying it. The will, or trust, stated that if the trustee wanted to get any kind of schooling—educational, physical, any betterment to develop themselves- the trustee could access the resources for such a request. It included anything to better themselves, and the necessary equipment, travel, accommodations, instructors, etc., to pay for it. All the recipients were required to do was to write a letter of request to the trust company and they would send the money, as long as it fit into the guidelines of the trust.

My imagination wandered. Let's say you wanted to go to school at Harvard. Within the will, the funds were available, in addition to your normal allotment per year. If you needed a house, so you could live near school, you could access those resources also. If you needed a private tutor to help you raise your grades, you could take the money out of the trust. The trust said that it would supply everything that you needed. You see where I am going with this?

> "And my God shall supply all your need according to His riches in glory by Christ Jesus."
>
> **Philippians 4:19**

I sat there thinking, "Wow! What if I wanted to learn to water ski?" I am being honest: I could take water skiing lessons and they would pay for it because it was for my physical wellbeing. So then I reasoned, "What happens if I decided I wanted to learn to water ski in the Bahamas?" Couldn't I get a home in the Bahamas, because, according to the trust, that was in line with where I deduced that I would learn the new skill?

I saw that the trust was all-inclusive! All that had to be proven was that it lined up with the trust. I sat there at 5:30pm in Monte Carlo, Monaco, and got a revelation. I got it from God! "It's all right here. It's all right here!" **Only I correlated this with the Bible.**

Many times, we just sit back at church as the pastor tries to give us a broad view of the trust, God's Word. Hypothetically, each person is allowed a standard amount per year, but then you have to go home and study to find out what else is available for your specific situation. Study and know what is in there, not just for you, but also for others around you that don't know yet.

It's great to have the basics, but there is so much more. If we'll search the Last Will and Testament (Bible) diligently, we can apply it to our lives to address these storms! Let's dig a little deeper past the basics. Let's learn how to live in victory in the midst of them.

The Bible has proclaimed over and over again that the darker the world gets, the brighter we get. We all have the privilege of sharing the Gospel. It's not time to be motivated by fear. We are to "let our light so shine before men ..." I'm not talking about, "This *little* light of mine, I'm going to let it shine ..." I'm thinking more like kicking on a million candle watt power spotlight in the pitch black.

> "Now thanks be to God who always leads us in triumph in Christ ..."
> **II Corinthians 2:14**

Always! He always causes us to triumph. As we're walking through these storms into the unseen and unknown, faith is required. This kind of faith knows that He is with us and declares it is possible to achieve the dream.

> "But without faith it is impossible to please Him, for he that comes to God must believe that He is, and that He is a rewarder of them that diligently seek Him."
> **Hebrews 11:6**

God gives us opportunities to please Him. He wants us to please Him more than anything. Even the way we look at the storm has a response. My response is not ,"I have to get into that faith stuff." My response is, "God is giving me another opportunity to believe in Him and I can please Him. He loves me! He's not saying, 'Here is a carrot. Here's a carrot! Think you can get it?'" He's giving us opportunities to believe Him! Instead of whining to God, we should say, "Father, how should I respond to this? What would you have me do?"

> "So Jesus answered and said to them, "Have faith in God. For assuredly, I say to you, whoever says to this mountain, 'Be removed and be cast into the sea,' and does not doubt in his heart, but believes that those things he says will be done, he will have whatever he says. Therefore I say to you, whatever things you ask when you pray, believe that you receive them, and you will have them. And whenever you stand praying, if you have anything against anyone, forgive him, that your Father in heaven may also forgive you your trespasses."
> **Mark 11:22–25**

"And whenever you stand praying, forgive" ... "If you have anything against anyone, forgive him." When you don't forgive, it nullifies the trust.

The most powerful piece I received when I was at the trust office was that the testament or the will is only good when the testator dies and then it can go into effect. Our Testator, however, died to put it into effect and then He came back to life. He is resurrected! And in our communication with Him, He can reveal to us how to access the Will for the best possible outcome. We can sit down with our Heavenly Father and say, "Lord, there is a storm coming. Are there any preparations I should make, ones I haven't considered yet?"

And then what happens? People recognize when you've overcome and ask, "How did you make it through that difficulty? How did you have so much peace? " And you'll be able to tell them that you walk with the Prince of Peace.

> "And the peace of God which surpasses all understanding, will guard your hearts and minds through Christ Jesus."
>
> **Philippians 4:7**

I've told you that I like storms and that they can even be fun. I realize that they can be destructive also. I've experienced all kinds. But some storms bring big waves that can be surfed or great snow for those of us that enjoy extreme sports. Remember, I was a surfer, windsurfer, skier and snowboarder. James 1:2 tells us "to count it all joy when you fall in various trials." That almost sounds like I am supposed to like the trial. No, not like it, but expect that something good will be produced from it, "knowing that the testing of your faith produces patience." (James 1:3)

When you know how to live in victory no matter the storm, the enemy realizes he can't strip you of your passion, delay your promotion, keep you from being extreme or steal your dream. You are motivated by God and no longer by fear.

"The entrance of His word brings light" (Psalm 119:30).

✝

CHAPTER 6

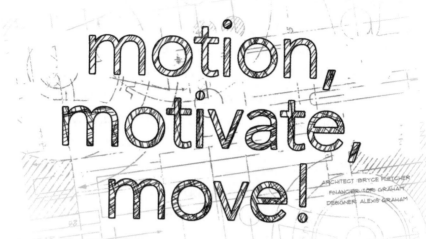

motion, motivate, move!

WHAT PUTS YOU IN YOUR GROOVE?

WHEN I WAS MUCH YOUNGER, there was this children's educational television show, "School House Rock"—it aired years and years ago. I don't remember watching the show but I do remember this catchy phrase from the show that they sang, "Conjunction, junction, what's your function?" Remember it??

We are calling this "Motion, Motivate, Move ... What Puts You in Your Groove?" Now it may sound funny, but many times your motive and motivation are critical ingredients to your success. The

Bible says in Proverbs 16:2: "All the ways of man are pure in his own eyes but the Lord weighs the spirits."

But *the Lord* weighs the spirits. Another translation says: "...but motives are weighed by the Lord." Have you ever heard people say, and it is almost a cliché, "Well, I know I should be doing this and that, but the Lord knows my heart." It's abundantly clear that they are not doing what they know in their hearts God is asking them to do. They may even be doing something radically different.

Such comments kind of let people off the hook don't they? "Well, God will excuse me because He knows my heart." Can't you see God with that quizzical or questioning look up there up in heaven looking down on our actions while we chat about our rationalizations?

It is like a mom that recognizes that her little kid has just pooped in his diaper, and then says, "Oh, my little baby just pooped in his diaper." I'm not trying to be crude, but you understand. Mom's say it, as the stink from the diaper rises for everyone to smell, " My little kid just pooped in his diaper, oh, isn't that nice?" No! It's not nice. It's a natural part of life as a baby, but something that we expect he will grow up and out of. But sometimes *we* do a similar thing and carry that a little too far, don't we?

Let's look at His Word, let's see what God says. Does God want a bunch of well-wishers who aren't successful? "Oh my, being a Christian is so tough. He already knows how much I love Him and He knows all the things that I **try** to do for Him."

Look with me at 1 Corinthians 15:57: "But thanks be to God who gives us the victory through our Lord Jesus Christ." Now that doesn't sound like, "Well I should be doing this, this, this and this, but God knows my heart." No, what is written is: "Thanks be to God who gives us the victory."

We can dig deeper by looking up the word "give" in the Greek to see what it means. It means: **to give, to bestow**. So if God has given the victory already, how does that connect with "Well, God knows my heart."?

If someone gives something, there must be a receiver. Maybe we aren't taking the victory He's already given. Victory is ours is great news. We just need to receive it!

Let's examine another reference: 2 Corinthians 2:14. Remember what Paul says, as directed by the Holy Spirit, "In the mouth of two or three witnesses let everything be established." "Now, thanks *be* to God…" I love that both of these scriptures begin with: "Now thanks *be* to God."

I think there is *something* in that thanksgiving part. It's the launching pad to triumph, victory and success. Does He "occasionally" lead us in triumph in Christ? Does He "once in a while" lead us in triumph in Christ? Or "every now and then He helps us succeed?" Sometimes He pushes us to the brink of success?

Listen, I know we all have struggles, I'm not trying to get down on anyone. But if He is always leading us in triumph, we can succeed. Success is knowing the will of God and doing it!

Let's use an allegorical illustration. We see our Lord here, He *leads* me, but I just stand there and don't make a move. He starts leading me to go somewhere else, but again, I don't make a move to *go* anywhere.

"Oh really, I have to do the walking?" Maybe we are not hitting **"triumph"** because we are not following His lead. "Thanks be unto God who always causes us to triumph in Christ … thanks be unto God who leads us in victory."

Now let's look at the heart. What's *in* the heart? "The motives are weighed by the Lord" (Proverbs 16:2). What do we call the heart? The "core," don't we?

It is the spirit, but we call it the core, the driving force in our lives. "He plays with all of his heart" or "He plays with his whole heart. He knows it by heart, she knows it by heart, she puts her whole heart into it." What's the heart? It's the thing that drives you, the thing that motivates you.

"Therefore judge nothing before the time until the Lord comes, who will both bring to light the hidden things of darkness and reveal the counsels of the heart. Then each one's praise will come from God" (1 Corinthians 4:5).

Now, let's look at this scripture in several other translations. The NIV says, "the motives of men's hearts." Right here, He is saying in 1 Corinthians 4:5, He is going to reveal the counsels *or* the motives of our heart! The Amplified version: "It exposes the motives of man's heart."

And the Message translation: "only then will each one's praise come from God. Only then will any one of us get to hear the 'well done' of God."

So why would God want to expose the motives of men's hearts? I would say probably because it is the root or the driving force in our lives. What's **the** root or what's **a** root? It is the basic cause, source, or origin of something. It is the essential substance or nature of something; the underground happenings. It starts down as a seed planted in the soil, its foundation, then it grows, develops and it's fruit emerges and then it ripens. The root is the stimulus, the incentive, the drive, its the spur of the seed planted. If God knows your heart and if the heart is the thing that motivates you, pushes you, drives you and causes you to do what you are doing, then He knows **you**.

Motivate means "to impel, to urge on, to drive forward, as if by exertion of strong moral pressure, to impart motion, to propel. Actually this one word, "motivate" has a synonym "move", which comes from "to dig." And where is the root? Underground. Look how motivate correlates to "dig."

Motion, motivate, move—what puts you in your groove? Groove is the niche situation suited to one's abilities or interests. What gets you 'top form' can also describe it. An enjoyable or exciting experience as in, "Oh, he has got his groove back!"

A pronounced enjoyable *rhythm!*

What does that sound like when I am talking about getting in your groove? Does that sound like John 10:10? "… Life and life more abundantly …"

HE KNOWS YOU BEST

When I was in Bible school, one of our instructors, Patsy Cameneti, had us pray regularly the Amplified version of Matthew 9:38: "Lord thrust out your laborers into your harvest!"

Two weeks to the day that I graduated from Bible school, I

was in the south of France. I didn't have the desire to go to cultured Europe. I wanted to go to Australia because I liked the idea of hanging out in the bush and the woods, the raw surf and the sharks and all that kind of fun stuff. I liked sleeping on the beach every now and then, you know, under the stars, not fancy five star hotels. Seriously!

I moved to Bible school from Hawaii, where all we wore were slippers for our daily footwear. Well, we called them "slippers." "Flip-flops" are probably what you call them. Shorts and T-shirts were optional. I taught wind surfing every day and I even surfed on my days off. That was my life. I expected that I would leave Bible school and go back to somewhere like that!

But when I went off to Bible school, my life was redirected. Just before leaving Hawaii, I had received a visa to travel to Australia. My plan was to start doing art on the streets, and to witness to surfers and surf.

Instead, God called me to Tulsa, Oklahoma. At the end of that adventure, I got an opportunity to travel to France to teach windsurfing. I never would have chosen France.

However, I am an artist and love art. I didn't care much about food since it had always been like fuel to me. I ate whatever kept me going, but French food was awesome, it was seriously fantastic food! And I loved the language, the people and the culture! The language was artistically pleasant to my ears!

After six months in France, I returned to the U.S. and found myself flying Pakistan International Airlines. There were two western people on the plane. I was sitting on an aisle seat and a French-American lady was sitting across from me.

I pulled out my Bibles to read. I had one of those little mini-bibles in English and another Bible in French. As per instructions from the pastor's mother in Nice, France. She was a linguist and had said that if you want to learn another language, read the Bible in the language that you want to learn and then compare it to the English version .

So while flying, I looked over and this French–American lady is reading a Bible! Finally, after two hours of flying, we started talking. She said, "Wow! Are you a Christian?" With two Bibles either I am truly a Christian or I am a religious scholar. Later, she said "I thought you were so spiritual because you were reading two Bibles."

" No, I am just trying to learn the language," I said.

In the course of our conversation, I explained that I would have never chosen France, I simply wanted to hang out and be a surfer, do some air brushing on the streets and preach to surfers about Jesus. But, I further explained, that the funny thing was how I came to love the French food, love the French language and love the art.

Almost prophetically, she responded: "God knew that. Because He created you, and He knew exactly what you would like."

God knew that France was a situation suited to my abilities, interests and an enjoyable or exciting experience. Motion, motivate, move—what puts you in your groove?! This isn't a vague, fuzzy concept about, "Oh, God knows my heart." Your heart is the thing that drives you, but the question is to where?

Maybe that's why God wants to expose people's hearts. I would rather get exposed in the beginning, so I get on track, instead of later thinking "Oh my gosh, I missed my whole life! What happened? Couldn't you have told me before?"

Yes! He can tell you beforehand but sometimes correction isn't super fun, is it?

God responds: "You are doing it the wrong way!"

"I am? This is the way I always did it, isn't that OK?"

"No! You are doing it the wrong way!"

"Can I continue trying it like this and see if it will get better?"

Do you know how Albert Einstein defined insanity? He called it doing the same thing over and over again and expecting different results. Isn't that kind of how we are sometimes? "I like the way I am doing things, even if it's not working for me, but can I keep doing this? Please!"

FALSE OR TRUE MOTIVES

The Bible says some people are out preaching Jesus for the wrong motives! Why does He want to expose our motives?

So He can condemn us and say, "You're bad! Bad!?" No! He doesn't want that!

> It is true that some preach Christ out of envy and
> rivalry, but others out of goodwill. The latter do so

in love, knowing that I am put here for the defense of the gospel. The former preach Christ out of selfish ambition, not sincerely, supposing that they can stir up trouble for me while I am in chains. But what does it matter? The important thing is that in every way, whether from false motives or true, Christ is preached.

Philippians 1:13–16

What will the end result be? These people are preaching Christ for the wrong reason and what do you think will happen? Do you think they are going to get a reward from God, if their motives are false?

"False motives or true?" Why would God want to expose our motives? What's motivating us and what makes us do what we are doing? What are they going to get for their reward?

Psalm 106:5 says of the Israelites, "God gave them the desire of their heart but He gave them leanness of soul!" They said, "We are tired of this manna stuff!" Everyone thinks that manna is such a descriptive name.

We relate it to proverbial heavenly nourishment. But do you know what it actually means? The definition is, "What is it?" or "What is that stuff?"

We use it endearingly, "Oh, I've got manna from heaven." Isn't that peculiar, where everyday words come from?

But the Israelites complained, "Oh! We had meat and all these other favorite foodstuffs." And so God gave them what they asked for, but He also gave them leanness of soul. They couldn't even enjoy the thing!

But when we do things from the right motive, it will satisfy us and others!

A minister friend, Tony Cameneti, said, "If your motives are wrong, you don't know where you are going" … and I add: *If you don't know where you are going, how are you going to get there?*

Think about it, we are talking about motives. Are they going to get rewarded? Or what reward will they get? **Leanness of soul? That seems to be the opposite of groove, doesn't it?** Have you ever received something that you wanted badly and it didn't satisfy you? Or conversely, you got what you wanted and it *did* satisfy you?

God wants you to have life, and life more abundantly! But I do believe that if our core, our heart, is going after it in the wrong manner, with the wrong motives, that it produces "leanness of soul." That doesn't sound like an enjoyable or exciting experience to me.

One summer I had the privilege of having Lewis travel with us, a twelve-year-old from Manchester, England. It was God's idea. I was sitting in a church service in the United Kingdom, minding my own business. I was scheduled to speak at a youth camp in a few days. I wasn't even speaking that service, but was simply sitting in the back of the church, and the Lord says, "I want you to take Lewis with you this summer." Two months, 8,000 miles, with a 12-year-old boy.

Lewis was a fun, crazy kid! He had never had a dad in his life, but "The goodness of God leads men to repentance (Romans 2:4). And He is a Father to the fatherless" (Psalm 68:5). The Lord said to me, "Would you like to take him for the summer?"

Well, when the Lord said that to me, I said, "Yes, Lord I would love to take him for the summer!" Lewis was like a human dynamo. He was up at six in the morning. "Let's play tennis!" Two hours later, "Let's go swimming! Let's go rollerblading! Let's ride bicycles!" It's 10 o'clock at night and it's, "Let's play chess!" I mean, he was truly a human dynamo!

Every night we read this book together, a British book entitled, "The Shock of Your Life." In it, people were coming before the throne of Jesus to be judged. As they stepped before the Lord, everything they had done was judged by fire. Ministers who did it for the wrong motive had a small reward, just little pieces of gold. Young people came before the throne who had been telling people about Jesus during their lifetime. People had thought they were crazy! Then they came to Jesus and these same young people would pick up this huge crown and place it before Jesus!

There were a couple of times when Jesus tried to take them to the next level. A girl wrote, "I was sitting in my room and I willingly sinned and I knew it wasn't making God happy." She said she looked back over her life and when she went before the throne, over in the corner of the room, Jesus sat at an architect-style table. The girl saw herself sitting on a couch while making a decision for the wrong reason. She watched as Jesus smiled, but not necessarily with pleasure.

You see, He had a big plan for all their lives including that girl's life. But she said when she made up her mind to sin, He rolled it [her life's plan] up and scaled down the drawing! And then she said, another time in her life when she willingly sinned again, then He scaled it down smaller! He still loved her and she made it to heaven but there were no rewards in heaven!

You think about that ... what do you want to have accomplished when you're done here? The Bible says in 2 Peter 1:3, "God gives all things that pertain unto life and godliness." He knows that we need clothes, food, housing and all. God knows that you need things that pertain unto life, but I also want to make clear to you, how important it is to follow His plan with the **right** motive.

THE MIND OF CHRIST

I learned about this when I moved from Hawaii to the Midwest and went to Bible College. I had been told some things about Rhema Bible Training College. I had been told Kenneth E. Hagin was teaching people to *be* like gods. Well, all I knew was just how to *follow* God.

I knew I was supposed to be there, but I was getting up every morning at 5:30am to pray in my closet before school, because I didn't want to be deceived.

Listen, I mean I was *in* my closet, literally singing to the Lord, had my Word out, praying in tongues. All because I didn't want to get deceived! Well, after a couple of months, I had a huge problem happen in my life. I lost my car, my apartment, and I lost my job.

These friends of mine had sold me a car that were against Kenneth Hagin Ministries. I wrote them a letter explaining how God had revealed to me that it was a good ministry. They responded and wrote, "We want our car back." They thought they were helping me—I mean they really, really thought they were helping me! And for years I was asking, "What happened God? I was seeking you, I was following you!"

Years later it came to me. I realized I was seeking Him for the wrong reason! You don't just want to love your wife because you are afraid to be alone, that's not a good motive of love. Sooner or later something else is going to fill that void.

That's why it is so important what our motives are! It took me, I believe, eight years before I understood what happened. But He revealed to me that I wasn't seeking Him for the *right* reason and He had to pull that root out! You might even disagree with me on my assessment of this. But can you see that I would have spent the rest of my life seeking Him so that I wouldn't be deceived? *How about seeking Him because I am so in love with Him*?!

I paid the price for a couple years, but I realized that God wanted to eliminate that root in my life. Sometimes we build things on the wrong foundation but God will help us get rid of it! Did you understand what I said? *Help us get rid of it!*

For what? So that it won't carry over for the rest of our life! If your motives are wrong, you don't know where you are going. As in my motive to seek God so that I wouldn't be deceived! One person that I know, shortly before she was born again, cried out to God when she was surrounded by jellyfish on a jet ski! For me, being a surfer in Hawaii, I sat on the beach and I said, "God, if You are up there, I want to know Who You are!"

I had an encounter with God on the beach in Hawaii. My life wasn't all grandeur, but I *was* sitting on a beach in Maui. "Are you up there?" It really started out in sort of a good way. Talk about the goodness of God!

Patsy Cameneti has said that people seek God for two reasons. One is caused by a great crisis in their life, "Oh God, please save me!" Or they get a touch of heaven and they can't do without it!

However you got saved, glory to God, you got saved! But you want His goodness to attract you—not every time there is a crisis, you run around, "Hey, please help me, please help me up! And then "Thank you God! Can I go on with my regularly scheduled life now?" Trouble comes again and, "Hey, please help me up, please, please!" Doesn't this make sense?

Where are our motives? **Survival verses triumphant victories.** Where do you want to be?

When I taught skiing, I got people that were novices that would ski down the hills and figure out only a little bit about how to ski. They were crazy! When I took them up to a steeper mountain, they went screaming down the hill out of control! They could hurt themselves and/or hurt others because they didn't have a good foundation.

We can build a solid foundation for ourselves. We can start right away, even if our motives are a little bit twisted. It's been said, "It's not how you start, it's how you finish."

But you need to find that "place of goodness" where you can quote Psalms 103:1–2, "Bless the Lord, oh my soul and all that is within me, bless the Lord oh my soul and forget not all His benefits." Start counting off all His benefits and you will see how wealthy, blessed, happy and to be envied you really are!

So now, let's get our groove back. **He is the God of second, third and fourth chances.** You say, "How do I get my groove back, how do I shift my motivation?" Philippians 2:3 says: "Let nothing be done through selfish ambition but in lowliness of mind, let each esteem each other better than himself. Or in the ESV," Let each one of you look out for not only his own interests but for the interests of others

Look with me at Philippians 3:15: "Therefore let as many as are mature have this mind." He said, "Have this mind …" Wait a minute, what if I have this *other* mind? He's telling us don't have that mind anymore! He is saying, "**You** change your mind!"

What is the link between the flesh and the spirit, the spirit and the flesh? It is our soul; our mind, will and emotions. If we don't ever feed our spirit man, our inner man, he is a little weakling in there. It doesn't matter how much we feed and exercise our body, even if we did it to the point where we could be Mr. Universe. Down there on the inside of us would be a little weak spirit person.

When your soul tries to choose between one or the other, who is going to be stronger? That's why Jesus said, "Man shall not live by bread alone, but by every word that proceeds from the mouth of God" (Matthew 4:4). He gave us the way to success.

Joshua 1:8: "This Word shall not depart from your mouth, but you shall meditate …"

Do you know what meditate means? It means to mutter, utter, speak, imagine, say. You should meditate day and night. There are 12 hours in the day and 12 hours in the night—I think thats a lot of time right there! God says "day and night," that you may observe to do according to all that is written therein, for then **you will** make your way prosperous and **you will** have good success.

"Let each of you look out not only for his own interests, but also for the interests of others. Let this mind be in you which was also in Christ Jesus" (Philippians 2:4–5). Change your mind. **You change it!** "And if anything you think otherwise, God will reveal it to you" (Philippians 3:15). Okay you say, "God I want to change my mind." When God revealed that to me, it took me a while to understand also.

"But God, I lost my car, I lost my apartment, I lost my job …" Could you see if that would have continued on years later, I would have still been seeking God out of fear. I was there. That's was me—I am talking about me!

But we can turn it around! The Bible says, "God doesn't give us a spirit of fear, but of power, love and a sound mind" (2 Timothy 1:7). "And if in anything you think otherwise God will reveal it to you" (Philippians 3:15). Another translation states: **"God will make this clear to any of you who are striving for other goals."** People seek God for many different reasons, so ask Him to make your reason clear to you. The first way is to spend time in the Bible. And not just reading and perusing it, but speaking the scripture out loud!

Motion, motivate, move—what puts *you* in *your* groove? What motivates *you* is your core, it's what's in *your* heart. It's the thing that drives you and critical ingredients to your success!

motion, motivate, move!

CHAPTER 7

samson generation

THE FIRST TIME I HEARD the term "Samson Generation," I was transcribing a section of a sermon by a respected minister. At the end of the sermon, another minister whom I didn't know, got hold of the microphone and was shouting about the current generation being a "Samson Generation," a generation raised from birth in the ways of the Lord. I kept ignoring it, but as I was listening to the audiotape, I couldn't help but hear this phrase repeatedly until it stuck back in the far recesses of my mind.

Finally, one day I succumbed and opened up my Bible and went to the book of Judges. Immediately I thought, "Yeah, that's it. Judges, that's what we need, a generation of judges to bring this dark world to account for their wickedness and evil ways." But as I looked at the margin of my Bible, the direction became clear in my puny mind.

"Champions" and "rescuers" was the meaning of the Hebrew word for Judges. Then I turned to Genesis 49:16 to research the tribe of Dan, and Jacob's last word "shall judge his people" were also rooted in "savior, champion" and "rescue."

Talk about revelation from God! A generation of champions and rescuers, having been raised from birth, with a knowledge of God, delivering His people from their destructive ways and even eternal destruction. A Samson Generation! We'll delve deeper to see if this doesn't parallel today's youth.

Let's look at Judges 13:1:

> "Again the children of Israel did evil in the sight of the Lord. And the Lord delivered them into the hands of the Philistines for forty years. And there was a certain man from Zorach of the family of the Danites whose name was Manoah and his wife was barren and had no children. And the angel of the Lord appeared to the women and said to her, 'Indeed now you are barren and you have bore no children but you will conceive and bear a son. Now therefore, please be careful not to drink wine or similar drink and not to eat anything unclean for behold you shall conceive and bear a son and behold no razor shall come upon his head for the child shall be a Nazarite for God from the womb and he shall begin to deliver Israel from the hand of the Philistines.'"

> So the woman came and told her husband, saying, "A man of God came to me and his countenance was like the countenance of the angel of God, very awesome! But I did not ask him where he was from and he did not tell me his name. And he said to me, 'Behold you will conceive and bear a son, now drink no wine or similar drink nor eat anything unclean for the child shall be a Nazarite to God from the womb till the day of his death.'"
>
> **Judges 13:1–7**

The Nazarites could not cut their hair and they had certain dietary laws that they followed, extremely strict rules to set themselves apart. If you were consecrated unto the Lord to be a Nazarite, then you had a different set of rules, you were separate, pulled away from the norm of others.

"Then Manoah [her husband] prayed unto the Lord."

> 'Oh my Lord, please let the man of God who you sent come to us again and teach us what we should do for the child to be born.' And God listened to the voice of Manoah and the angel of God came to the women again as she was sitting in the field. But Manoah, her husband was not with her. Then the women ran in haste and told her husband and said to him, "Look the man who came to me the other day has just now appeared to me."
>
> **Judges 13:8–10**

So Manoah arose and followed his wife. And when he came to the man he said to him, 'Are you the man who spoke to the woman? And He said, "I am." And Manoah said, "Now let your words come to pass, what will the boy's rule of life and his work?"

Judges 13:11–12

And the angel of the Lord repeats this again to Manoah. "Of all that I said to the woman let her be careful. She may not eat anything that comes from the vine nor may she drink any wine or similar drink nor eat anything unclean, all that I command her, let her observe."

Judges 13:11–14

In verses 15 and 16, we see that they believed it was a man from God visiting them and so they offered to share their meal. They didn't quite understand who the visitor was. He convinced them to sacrifice the goat instead, and, as they did, the angel ascended in the flame to God. "For Manoah didn't know He *was* the Angel of the Lord" (Judges 13:16).

Let's examine this text. Notice that she was given the instructions from the angel twice because they are difficult instructions to follow. We don't just hear them once but we hear them twice. Let's say someone gives you instructions to a great restaurant. They tell you to go out of your driveway and turn onto Eccles Road by pulling out to Langworthy and then make the right and you'll be on Eccles Road. When you make the right and go down the street, you'll see China Sea and they've got really good Chinese food.

But if I was trying to go out to the main road, and someone gave me directions to Chiffon Street, then I would have to go another way. I would have to go down to Liverpool Street and then make a right on the A5066 and then switch over 0.6 miles ahead to the A666 and then jump over to the A4592 and then ... you understand what I am talking about? Now we are getting into complicated, specific and detailed directions.

So why do you need specific directions? Because it is a difficult road to travel! If directions are easy, you say, "Go out there, make a right and you are there." But if you have specific, detailed directions, it may be a difficult road to travel.

Youth today have a difficult road to travel and God has specific directions for them because it's a narrow way. The way is not a wide, broad path. When youth take the broad way, as Jesus called it, it means that many will be veering off. Most of them don't even realize it. They haven't had the life experience that older people have had, they haven't seen some of the things we have seen. They have seen a lot more than we ever did in some areas, as in loss of innocence most likely, but not in experience.

The first thing the angel did was give Manoah specific direction. He set them apart with specific directions. You might say, "What? How does that pertain to me? I'm not a youth. Do I need specific directions?" Manoah prayed to the Lord, in verse 8, "Oh my Lord please let the man of God who you sent come again and teach us what we should do for the child to be born." He's saying, "Hey, tell me the directions again for my child."

"And God listened to the voice of Manoah and the angel of the Lord came again" (Judges 13:9). Now watch how this unfolds. Manoah rose and followed him and said, "Are you the man who spoke to this woman? Now let your words come to pass, what will be the boy's rule of life and his work?" And look what the angel of the Lord said. He said to the woman, "she may not eat anything that comes from the vine." Twice he gave directions to the mother

You shouldn't expect your kids to develop in areas that you haven't. Like produces like. The apple doesn't fall far the tree. You have got to follow the directions so your kids follow the directions.

Your youth see you say, "Hallelujah, bless the Lord! Oh I am right here with you Father!" And then they see you at home, "Oh, I can't believe this @#$&*." Or they see you blessing the pastor, "Oh, Pastor it's so good to see you!" Then they see you back in the kitchen, "Gosh, I don't like the glasses he wears!" And I won't go any further with other insults said.

If you want to see your kids live for Jesus Christ, then you have got to have a solid path for them to follow! When I was a ski instructor, I couldn't take my students places I had never been before. I can tell them about it! "Oh you should ski this black diamond, it is so awesome ..."

I can give them the right technical terms and tell them what to do in theory. But if I can't demonstrate for them, what example do they have to follow? They might learn the buzzwords: deep, steep, powder, bumps, etc. but cannot understand how to apply the lesson.

Do you know what you get when that happens? You get spectators. You don't get participants. You get people that are not involved but they know cool phrases. "Oh, bless you brother, bless you sister. Hallelujah! The joy of the Lord is my strength." Then at home you are beating your head up against the wall, "How am I going to get an answer from God on this?"

God gives the directions first to the parents. You have to live the life first, if you really expect your kids to follow. They are going to watch your example more than they are going to listen to your words. Let's let our words line up with our example. Let's do it! Let's develop champions and rescuers!

First thing was that Samson was set apart and given specific directions. The second thing was he had strength beyond himself. "When the Gazites were told Samson has come here and they surrounded the place and laid in wait all night at the gate of the city. They were quiet all night saying, 'In the morning when it is day we will kill him" (Judges 16:2).

"And Samson lay low until midnight, then he arose at midnight, took hold of the doors of the gate of the city" (Judges 16:3a). Now this is the gate of the city! And it says, "The gate of the city and the two pulled them up bar and all, put them on his shoulders and carried them to the top of the hill that faces Hebron" (Judges 16:3b). Listen, I don't care if it was only 10 feet high! This is a man ripping up the gates of the city and walking out with them. I've traveled in the Middle East and, from what I've seen there, I don't think they were little gates. I'm sure they wanted everybody to know, "We are the Gazites." I think they were some large gates. He had strength beyond himself!

Now then in Judges 15:15: "Samson finds a fresh jaw bone of a donkey, reaches out his hand, takes it and kills a thousand men with it!" This was a powerful man under the anointing. Picture Jackie Chan taking out more than 25 men at a time with sticks, weapons and anything he could get his hands on. But Samson, an untrained fighter as far as we know, took out 1,000 men armed with the jawbone of a donkey. I am not saying your kids are going to kill 1,000 men. Just that he had strength beyond his natural ability.

Third, he did really unusual things. The Samson Generation is doing unusual things. Judges 14:6: "The spirit of the Lord came mightily upon him." Well, look at this in verse 5, "And to his surprise a young lion came roaring against him and the spirit of the Lord came mightily upon him and he tore the lion apart as one would have torn apart a young goat."

You know, like we all do. Isn't this what it says? "As one would have torn apart a young goat ..." How many of you guys have ever torn apart a young goat? It is nothing, is it? You know, just as I rip a piece of paper, I rip a young goat. This is unusual.

It says he basically rips apart a lion! Now it says throughout the Bible that the lion is the fiercest animal. A lion is one of the strongest land animals and it is very, very vicious. It's not as if it's simply, "Meow, meow. Hey, kitty, kitty." So he does really unusual things, doesn't he?

In Judges 14:12–13, in preparation for his wedding feast, Samson said to them, "Let me pose a riddle to you. If you can correctly solve and explain it to me within seven days of the feast then I will give you thirty linen garments and thirty changes of clothing but if you can not explain it to me then you should give me thirty linen garments and thirty changes of clothing."

Then he gives this riddle to these guys and then, it gets really intense. His future wife coaxes the answer and betrays him so he has to remit the thirty changes of clothes. Then another time he catches 300 hundred foxes, ties them tail to tail, puts torches between them and sends them through the olive groves, vineyards and cornfields.

Now listen, if you just tied one or two foxes together, put torches between them and let them go in the backyard that would be pretty strange, let alone tying 300 of them together! I'm clarifying my point—he did unusual things. I am talking about a Samson Generation. They'll be doing unusual things, because we are in an unusual time.

Let's reiterate the points. First thing, he was set apart with specific directions. You say, "What? I don't have specific directions. Should I go back to Numbers and grow my hair real long and follow these dietary laws?" No, not unless God tells you to, then you should. I will give you some specific directions in scripture. 1 Peter 2:9: "But you are a chosen generation, a royal priesthood, a holy nation." One version says, "A people of His own." The King James says, "a peculiar people." When you study this, it means purposeful, peculiar and possession in motion. A possession in motion advancing—this is the Samson Generation! We are His special, peculiar people!

We have been called out of darkness and into His marvelous light. We once were not even a people but are now the people of God. Hallelujah! We are not desperate anymore! Hope lives on the inside of us. We've obtained mercy! (1 Peter 2:9–11). He describes us as "beloved" and then He gives us actual instructions to follow: "I beg you as sojourners and pilgrims, temporary residents and foreigners, abstain from fleshly lusts which war and against the soul. Having your conduct honorable among the Gentiles" (1 Peter 2:11–12). Your conduct shouldn't be honorable just in front of the Christians, but your conduct should be honorable in front of the unsaved.

Don't go into your work place and tell those inappropriate jokes. "Hey, did you hear the one about …" And then you get that little check in your heart, but then they laugh so you come up with another joke.

Our conversation honorable, our lifestyles honorable, "… that when they speak against you as evil doers they may by your good works which they observe, glorify God in the day of exhibition [or visitation]"(1 Peter 2:12). They are going to need an example, too. "Therefore submit yourself to every ordinance of man for the Lord's sake, whether to the king or supreme …" (1 Peter 2:13).

He is giving you instructions! If you need instructions, they are right here! You can start right here! "For this is the will of God that by doing good you may put to silence the ignorance of foolish man, as free yet not using liberty as a cloak for vice, but as bond servants for God" (1 Peter 2:14–15). Instructions continue, "Honor all people, love the brotherhood, fear God, fear the emperor" (1 Peter 2:17). "You are a chosen generation," Hallelujah! We love that! "We are peculiar, unusual, special, look at us!" But then He lays it out how you are going to do that. It looks different because the world is going one way and you are going the other way.

So a quick recap: First, he was set apart with specific directions; second, he had strength beyond himself; and third, he did unusual things. The package is perfect! Just because it is an unusual time, God has made you different and you are living on the edge doesn't mean you have to live so far over, into the world's way, that you fall into it!

Kenneth Hagin Jr. says, "Go into every man's world!" The Bible says go into all the world, the entire world. He needs His people everywhere. He needs people that are doctors and lawyers. He also needs funky and unusual people. Most importantly, whatever we are, He needs us to stay close to Him!

Let me explain further with a message I heard about Samson by Oral Roberts. He was talking about the wagon train days. The story was about a wagon master recruiting people to drive the wagons to deliver the mail. He put out this flier and men came looking for work. A young man, about 15–16 years old, showed up. The day they were recruiting, the young man showed up again, sat down and listened to all the men brag.

"Yeah, I have taken Donner Pass out there before. We went through Donner Pass and that wagon I drove had six horses. I had one wheel off on the edge and was slipping off on the side."

Then the next guy said, "Yeah, you should have seen me. I had two wheels off on the Pass. We were coming around that corner, you know Deadman's Curve, where you are coming around the bend …" And then another man, "Yeah I had the one horse running on the edge and the whole wagon was off the back."

Each man was trying to outdo the other, bragging about how precarious their situation was, you know, like men do. This young man walked up and said to the wagon master, "Sir, can I take back my application?" And the wagon master asked, "Why?"

The young man said, "Well sir, uh, I know how to drive a wagon, but I wouldn't drive it like those guys drive it, dangerous like." Explaining further he said, "I would hug the mountain as close as I could, because we're already on the edge."

Similarly, people don't realize what can happen when you slip off the edge in your Christian walk. The people who have been watching your life, they could possibly slip off with you. And when He sends you to be at the forefront, to be a pioneer, a spearhead, if it goes the wrong way, the whole spear follows.

Are you (or the kids in your life) doing things that are a little bit unusual? How do you know if it is right in their eyes or if it is just out there? If it lines up with the "Direction Book!" When I travel on the road, I am like a little kid, "Let me see the map! Where are we right now on the map?"

This is why you do this! Inquire of the Holy Spirit, "Where am I on the map? Are we there yet? Are we there yet?" I am doing that in the Spirit, are you? "Are we there yet? Are we there yet?" Listen, there is a better place than this place on earth! We are pilgrims and sojourners. We're just passing through this place. We have another passport from a foreign country! Heaven is our homeland!

Maybe you are thinking, "I'm not a youth and I don't have any children of my own." How does this involve me? I dare say that you are influencing someone with your decisions, your lifestyle, your dreams, your career, your calling and your conversation. People are always watching others, paying attention to their actions and reactions. My last story is a great example of such.

When I was a ski instructor, I had a three-year-old as a student. The ski school directors told us as ski instructors that it wasn't advantageous to teach somebody under the age of five. If you wanted to hire me as a private lesson all day long it was hundreds of dollars. The parents hired me six hours with a three-year-old, but a three-year-old doesn't have muscle memory to retain hundreds of dollars worth of lessons. The parents said, "Our Max Lyon from Newport Beach has energy! I said, "It's your money, I'm just working for the ski resort."

I was skiing with Max and taught him to do a little wedge, just the basics of skiing. He was progressing so we took a little trail. As he came swooshing down the mountain, he got to the bottom of the trail and declared, "I'm a winner!" He did! He threw both hands in the air and screamed, "I'm a winner!"

I looked at him and thought, 'Max Lyon didn't learn that by himself.' Max Lyon's parents must say to him when he does something right, "You are a winner, you are a champion, that's who you are Max Lyon!" And you know what? Max Lyon skied with me that day for six hours!

I dare say some of you couldn't ski with me for six hours! When I ski with me for six hours, I am tired. At the end of the day, we brought him in and he wrestled with his seven-year-old sister. There is life in being a winner! There is life in that! He was a child and he was strong at three years old!

Here is what I am going to ask you to do. One year at the end of youth camp, we had the youth pray for the adults. But the next year when I taught about the Samson Generation, I asked the parents and leaders to lay their hands on the youth and call them "champions" and "rescuers"! As I mentioned earlier, do you remember who the Danites were? Manoah was part of that tribe. They were actually prophesied over by Moses and Jacob (Israel), that they would be "judges" and "rescuers."

We need to speak words of life into our young people and into this generation! We need to lift our voices and call them (or yourself) champions and rescuers. Champions and rescuers!

> "Father, we lift up our young people (and their leaders) in the name of Jesus. We call them champions, rescuers and winners. We call them winners in Christ Jesus! Father, I thank You, for You said 'decree a thing and it will be done, it shall be established for you.'"
>
> **Job 22:28**

And it is. It is true. Our young people truly are champions, rescuers and winners. Called to plan and prepare, to dream and do and to lead and love. We are to make an impact on a world looking for Jesus. They shouldn't have to look far since He lives in you!

To summarize, no matter what your passion may be, how you have prepared for it, the extreme lengths you have gone for it, the difficulties you have weathered for them, the way you have cared for them or how you have used your influence, know that today is either the continuation of great adventures or a new beginning. You have been challenged and now have new possibilities before you. Today you choose the direction of your life. Start small, start big, but start. Nothing will ever change until you do!

ARCHITECT BRYCE FLETCHER
FINANCIER TORI GRAHAM
DESIGNER ALEXIS GRAHAM

CLIFF WAS BORN in Los Angeles, California, to an intellectual father and a mother from Colorado who adored her husband. They started an idyllic life nearby Griffith Park where they actually lived on Harmony Street.

Catholicism was semi-practiced in their home, meaning they definitely went to church on Christmas and Easter. He and his siblings attended private parochial school, which afforded a peer group that attended Mass on a more consistent basis. Cliff had a few interesting encounters with priests and nuns, ones that had experienced a real relationship with God. They left impressions, but nothing to anchor him, or so he thought.

After his parents rocky marriage ended with a physical altercation, Cliff had nightmares that lasted until he was about 14 years old. His father had "too much going on in his head" was one professional's diagnosis. Notably, his biological father was not a physical man—neither of athletic or violent nature—so it was presumably counterintuitive which caused this lasting impression to stay with him.

His mother remarried a finish carpenter/side job contractor when Cliff was seven, a man who worked long hours to provide for the family, sometimes even near the border of Mexico, but drank regularly. It was during these times that he physically corrected Cliff, which by today's standards, would be classified as abuse. One positive life lesson learned from his stepfather was the meaning of hard work.

When Cliff was 14 his mother and stepfather divorced. He excused this as an opportunity to lash out at life. This downward spiral lasted through his attempt to move to O'ahu, Hawaii, at 17. He stayed there about a week or so, until his aunt and uncle bailed him out, paying for his ticket home to California. His uncle treated him like a long lost son, as he had two younger daughters, but Cliff over-exercised his freedoms once again and was ejected from his new home. He moved into a prestigious neighborhood in the surrounding Los Angeles area where he rented a small quarter in a huge sprawling estate and found himself in more "freedom excesses."

Finding his way to Hawaii, this time Maui, Cliff put his hard-working skills to use as a windsurf instructor and spent most of his free time surfing. It was during this time that God began to draw him, and clearly revealed Himself to Cliff.

Over the next several years, Cliff was dramatically touched by the tragic deaths of several acquaintances, friends and even a close relative. The first, Johnny Powell, a surfing friend from Maui died hang-gliding while trying to overcome a marijuana dependency. Brad Lewis, a top rated surfer on the island, died when his truck collided on a dirt road with a Sugar Cane hauling truck, mercilessly decapitating him.

Another, Justin R., a talented young surfer that Cliff had known since Justin was 12, broke truancy school laws on the island of Maui. A judge sent him to a Door of Faith men's camp where he had an encounter with Christ only to quickly return to his old habits. He was killed shortly thereafter in a car accident while a part of surfing contests in California.

Still another encounter occurred with a gymnast from Urbana, Wisconsin that ended up visiting a surfing hostel on the North Shore of Hawaii. Cliff had been living on the North Shore at the end of the winter surfing season and gave the gymnast a word of knowledge, which she initially denied, but later professed as accurate. Through mail correspondence from her parents, Cliff later found out she had committed suicide on Halloween night. Others living too short of a life on earth exposed him to the radical awareness of a thief ending young people lives, as recorded in John 10:10, "The thief comes to kill, steal and destroy, but Jesus came that we might have life and that more abundantly."

A "chance" encounter with Jeannie, a one-to-one instructional Evangelist, opened new opportunities and the rest is history. Jeannie invited him to be her aide at a Christian business conference with Bob Harrison and Norvel Hayes. There, Cliff had a life-changing encounter with the Fire of God wherein Cliff was directed to attend Bible School in Oklahoma, now known as Rhema Bible College. He left school armed with faith and with his already adventurous spirit headed to the South of France for a six-month internship.

Now, over 20 years since that first trip to France, Cliff ministers the Good News around the world, from the deserts of the Middle East to the California coast and everywhere in between. As his wife puts it, he is a sort of Indiana Jones, Iron Man, Apostle Paul and James Bond mix. He is a faith-filled guy who will stir your dreams, encourage your faith and challenge you to reach the lost.

what is saved?

SAVED. SALVATION. BORN AGAIN. In today's politically correct climate these can be potentially arrogant and foolish words to utter, let alone adhere to.

But nonetheless, Jesus came to die for your sins. His claims either equate Him with God or are the ravings of a madman. There is no middle ground.

'All have sinned and fall short of the glory of God.' Romans 3:23

Romans 6:23 takes it further, 'For the wages of sin is death, but the gift of God is eternal life in Jesus Christ our Lord.'

Allow me to use a rudimentary analogy to explain the wound left by sin. As a young person, let's say you lift a twenty-dollar bill out of your mother's purse without her consent just as you walked out the front door. When you leave you turn and see the pain as she realized her child just stolen from her. It wouldn't matter if you had a hundred dollar bill in your pocket to replace the money, it could not purchase the trust you had just forfeited.

God knew our nature after the fall. So He made a way. Jesus hung on a tree and became the curse that scourged us to hell for eternity.

He basically made a switch.

And when we receive Him into our hearts and accept the sacrifice, the Bible says we are saved. We become the righteousness of God or in right-standing with God and He doesn't see our sin anymore.

He sees the sacrifice made by His only Begotten Son.

Romans 10:9-10…'that if you confess with your mouth the Lord Jesus and believe in your heart that God has raised Him from the dead, you will be saved.' He died in our place and then demonstrated God's power over death by rising from the grave.

Very simply when we believe this and confess Him as Lord, the

Bible unequivocally states we are born again. You become a new creation literally according to 2 Corinthians 5:17.

You are not guaranteed tomorrow. The Bible says 'Today is the day of Salvation'. Don't put it off until another day. If your house were burning you wouldn't want to wait and try to take care of it at a more opportune time.

It's a simple prayer but the most life changing, literally.

Pray this with me: ***Jesus, I believe you died on the cross for me to pay the price for my sin. Forgive me for my sins. I believe You were resurrected from the dead and are alive! Come into my heart, rule and reign in my life from this day on.***

If you have prayed this with me then according to Acts 2:21, 'Anyone who calls on the name of the Lord will be saved.'

Please contact us and let us know you have made this decision, we would like follow up with some information.

If you would like to contact Cliff Graham, please visit:
www.UnisonHarvest.com

or write:
Unison Harvest International
P.O. Box 818
Malibu, CA 90265 USA

or phone:
(310) 919-2803